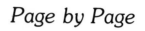

Page by Page

Page BY Page

by RUTH PAGE

Edited and with an Introduction by
ANDREW MARK WENTINK

The manuscripts of the essays and the visual items published in *Page by Page* are contained in the Ruth Page Collection housed in the Dance Collection, The New York Public Library, Astor, Lenox and Tilden Foundations. The extraordinary scope of Miss Page's life and career in American and international dance are documented in thousands of letters, business records, films, photographs, costume and set designs, books, clippings, scrapbooks, music scores (in the Music Division), and posters donated by Miss Page to The New York Public Library. Individual items in the collection are cataloged in detail in the *Dictionary Catalog of the Dance Collection.* A printed guide to the Ruth Page Collection will soon be published by The New York Public Library.

Our thanks to the following for permission to reprint articles which originally appeared in their publications: *Dance Magazine, Opera News, The New York Times* © 1937/40 by The New York Times Company; and to Time, Inc. for permission to reproduce the cover of *Time* for October 31, 1955.

ISBN 0-87127-102-8

Library of Congress Catalog Card Number 78-65648

Printed in the United States of America

Dance Horizons, 1801 East 26th Street, Brooklyn, N.Y. 11229

To
Margot Fonteyn —
"Marigoula" —
artist,
sea nymph,
friend.
—"Ruthaki"

Table of Contents

List of Illustrations

Author's Note

As you will soon see, I am not a writer, and only a few of these articles were written for publication. I don't know why I wrote many of them except that I felt the need to say certain things about certain people and events. Everything changes so fast in the dance world that some of these ideas now seem quaint. But here they are, for what they are worth! If it had not been for Andrew Wentink, these scribblings, accumulated over the years, would now be in the wastebasket.

—R.P.

Introduction

When offered the opportunity to be editor of these writings of Ruth Page, I was immediately faced with the problem of *how* to edit them. After careful examination and a growing familiarity with the author as well as the work, the answer became clear—Ruth Page *cannot* be edited! To revise the extemporaneous outpourings of this extraordinary personality is to divest it completely of the artistic impulsiveness, the creative restlessness, the vibrant sensuality, and the ingenuous audacity that render it so unique. Like the ballets, the written work captures the cultured intelligence, sophisticated wit, captivating charm, blithe geniality, and fresh originality of its author. These essays vary as much in their regard for traditional literary convention—from historical articles to sketchy but stinging epithets—as they do in subject matter, be it dance in Japan circa 1934 or a dog's life on the French Riviera.

However, at the core of each is the clear-sighted vision of a highly individualistic artist who, in more than half a century, has changed very little in her ability to speak frankly and with conviction. It seems that no one ever told Ruth Page how *not* to tell the truth, and the effect of one of her pithy, rather blasé observations of how it was (or is), is like seeing the smoke settle after the blast of a cannon.

Collected here for the first time, basically unchanged with only extensive repetitions deleted, are most of the written observations of Ruth Page's incredible life and career. Despite the chronological or alphabetical arrangement of articles within each section, the order is ultimately arbitrary. The vivid imagery and free association of ideas (sometimes spanning decades in one sentence) gives each composition an inherent poetic logic that resists the restrictive methods of constructing conventional prose. Therefore, the title of an essay often will suggest merely the starting point for a discussion that, like informal conversation, defines itself as it goes along. Occasionally, the rapid transitions from the original subject to the conclusion leaves the reader bewildered, but what appears to be fragmentary narrative is really sketchwork representing the vast experience and knowledge recorded by an amazingly quick and clever mind. The pieces of a life eventually fall into place as they do when making

Autobiographical Musings [ca. 1938]

So many Russian dancers have written their autobiographies, and the famous government dancing schools of Moscow and Leningrad have been described so many times, that we know more or less how every Russian dancer was trained. All these children received exactly the same schooling in dance as in everything else. When their school education was completed, they all made their debuts in about the same way—they became members of the corps de ballet or soloists, lived their lives dancing, and retired at the proper age on pensions. In other words, there was a *system* for dancers, and this system continues exactly the same under the Soviet regime as it did under the czars.

America has unquestionably produced many fine dancers and I think it is interesting to see how these dancers were able to make careers without any formalized system of education, with no company to go into, with no developed audience of dance lovers—with nothing, in other words, but their flaming ambition to dance. I am, I think, a fairly representative American dancer. I am in the middle of my career and have been closely associated with many of the most interesting dance figures of this age, and therefore I think the story of my life should be interesting as a study of the past fifteen years of dance history in America . . .

The earth didn't tremble, the gods didn't sing, there was no strange fluttering of wings and no mystical silence when I entered the world. I was quite an ordinary, dark-haired, black-eyed baby born in an ordinary house in an ordinary town in the Middle West. Indianapolis was dull, my friends were conventional, everything around me was so commonplace that at an early age I felt the need to soar, to dream, to fly away.

My mother and father, however, were not ordinary. My mother was born in Terre Haute, Indiana, of a German father, Louis Heinly, and a French mother, Genevieve Latour Watson. Her mother died when she was born and her father, who was a successful and well-to-do businessman, remarried and had many children. As my mother showed a talent for music at an early age, and as her childhood in Vincennes,

3

(Above): Marian Heinly Page. *(Above right):* Ruth Page in *To a Wild Rose*. *(Below):* The Page Family; Mother, Lafayette, Father, Irvine, Ruth, ca. 1902. *(Right):* Irvine, Mother, Lafayette, Father, Ruth, 1911.

4

Indiana, and Danville, Illinois, was not very happy, she was sent to Germany at sixteen to study music. She stayed there for five years studying piano in Leipzig. She wanted to be a concert pianist, but she met my father and they were married in Geneva, Switzerland, and that was the end of her career.

They returned to Indianapolis, and my mother has had an active part in the musical life of the city ever since. She had always been a whirlwind of emotion and energy. She raised three children, kept up her music, managed musical clubs and concerts, made her own dresses and mine, led an active social life, read vociferously, did her own gardening, played golf, and managed her household. I can never remember my mother being idle for a second during the day, and except for the ten-minute nap which she always took after lunch, she was a constant perpetuum mobile.

I have one brother, Lafayette, three years older than I, and another brother, Irvine, a year younger. My mother was carrying me during the time that Ona B. Talbot and she were organizing the first Indianapolis symphony orchestra, and, as they had to have all the meetings at our house on account of me, I was always called the Symphony Orchestra Baby.

My father was quite different from my mother. As opposed to her lightness, speed, and restlessness, he was slow and quiet and had infinite poise. He was born in Columbia, Kentucky, the youngest of a family of twelve children. He comes from the distinguished Page family of Virginia, his father having moved from Virginia to

Kentucky. His antecedents were English, Irish, Scotch, and Welsh, and this, mixed with the French and German blood on my mother's side, I suppose makes me the typical American.

My father became a distinguished nose, throat, and ear specialist beloved by all his patients and adored by all his friends for his southern charm, his genial wit, his inspiring philosophical conversation, and his sympathetic manner—a true southern gentleman of the old school. My father devoted all the later years of his life to establishing the James Whitcomb Riley Children's Hospital. This is one of the best children's hospitals in the country, and its existence is due entirely to the hard work of my father. He took me all over the state with him on his money-raising campaigns, and I always remember his theory that if he got money for the children's hospital, there would be a great deal less spent on insane asylums. The hospital was his great ambition, and I am happy that he lived to see his dream come true.

Father adored poetry and liked it for breakfast. So every morning we would learn poems and recite them at the breakfast table. My mother liked to read aloud, so every evening she would read to us from Dickens, Tolstoy, and countless other classics. I needed music to put me to sleep, so every night Mother would sit downstairs and play the piano till I fell asleep. As I write about this, it sounds like Utopia: poetry for breakfast, reading after dinner, music before bed. But our childhood wasn't so peaceful as it sounds. We were all hot-tempered, quarreled a great deal, and lived always with great excitement. My brother Lafayette wanted to be a great athlete, my brother Irvine wanted to be a great scientist, and I wanted to be a great dancer. So with footballs, baseball bats, banners, cups, microscopes, strange bottles, insects, seaweeds, toe shoes, tarletons, and theatrical makeup, we were a grand mixture of everything. And as we never agreed on any subject, there was constant arguing and tempestuous goings-on.

In the summer we usually went to Hyannisport on Cape Cod, where we had a little house by the sea. We were divinely happy and carefree there. Father would get up every morning gay as a lark. Mother gave me piano lessons. I loved to practice and to play, and I think if my hands had not been so small, I might have become a pianist instead of a dancer. We all loved music, and every night we used to beg mother to play us to sleep. I particularly like Tchaikovsky's *Andante Cantabile*, and that was my favorite piece to put me to sleep. Mother read to us almost every night. Our little friends would come in and mother used to read to us from the classics: Dickens, Tolstoy, Austen. We played by the sea all day long—my brother Irvine would come in with strange seaweeds and crabs and fish. We used to pick wild berries in the woods, and if we sold enough of them we thought we would be able to buy a yacht like the ones that kept coming to Hyannisport.

The days were golden and joyous, and I loved the sea passionately. I always have a longing to return to the sea—the little boats in the harbor, the strange exciting smells, the soft caressing air, the peace that comes with the sea, the smell of the pine woods, the simplicity of Cape Cod. I was infinitely happier in the summer than in the winter.

I was a child with longings for the moon, and I could never be happy because I never even came within reach of it.

The Russian Ballet [1916]

Diaghileff Ballet Russe, 1916.
Identifiable are Adolph Bolm, Serge Grigoriev, Leonide Massine, Serge Diaghileff and Lydia Lopokova.

Many Americans have been disappointed in the Diaghileff Ballet. Of course they cannot help but realize that it is a wonderful organization, but they do not understand it. They go once, are a little disappointed, and therefore never go again. No wonder they are not more enthusiastic. The Russian ballet is a thing that has to be studied, a thing that grows with knowledge of it. Some of the ballets are like Wagner operas, they have to be studied and seen time and again before they can be fully appreciated.

Thamar is one of these. The first time I saw it, I could only take in part of the colorful costumes and the dancing — the rest did not make much of an impression. About a week later I saw it again, and then the superb music, the silent tragedy and the color of the spectacle struck me . . .

The majority of people would go to see Karsavina or Pavlova, while they would never go to see the Diaghileff Ballet. It is just the opposite in Europe. Nijinsky tried a tour there with his own company, and it was an absolute failure, although he is without a doubt the most popular dancer in Europe. This seems very strange to us. However, Diaghileff has one man who is a really great artist, although he has not yet acquired a big reputation. This Adolf Bolm shows true genius. In the interpretations of his numerous roles he shows himself a really great actor. His remarkable vitality and vigor are shown to best advantage in *Prince Igor,* a ballet which seems to me to be a true expression of the Russians.

Although all of the men are excellent there are only two women worthy of special note, Lydia Lopokova and Flore Revalles. The former is a sweet, lovely, airy dancer for ballets like *Les Sylphides* and *L'Oiseau de Feu,* while the latter's talent lies chiefly in her acting. Flore Revalles, with her cold sensuality and oriental grace makes a beautiful Thamar, although her Zobeide in *Scheherazade* is not really so good. Despite the scarcity of individual dancers, the "tout ensemble" is so perfect that they are scarcely missed.

No one ever thinks of the Russian ballet without thinking of Bakst, the great color artist. Indeed, without this great master, the ballet would lose a great deal of its individualism. The minute the curtain rises on one of his scenes, you are immediately carried into whatever atmosphere he wishes to suggest. For instance, in *L'Après-midi d'un Faune,* how suggestive of nymphs and fauns is the curious mystic woods. Again in *Cléopâtre,* the very palace itself suggests the cold cruelness of its queen.

The music is by no means merely a detail of this wonderful organization, but forms almost its greatest beauty. Rimsky-Korsakov is as much a color artist in music as Bakst is in painting. By the overtures that the orchestra plays before the curtain rises, one could almost tell what is going to happen. The Russian ballet is grateful to Debussy and Chopin also for the music to two of its loveliest ballets.

By next year, America will probably begin to appreciate the Diaghileff Ballet. At present, it is a very curious sensation for M. Diaghileff, used to such success, to receive such a reception in America.

Serge Oukrainsky—
A Character Sketch [1916]

Virginia Treat, Eleanor Shaler, Ruth Page and Serge Oukrainsky, 1915.

At last rehearsal was over, and everybody had left but two men. These two were carrying on a very animated conversation—what it was all about I'm afraid no one but they knew. It sounded like two cats hurling x, y's and z's at each other—at least so the Russian language sounded to me. I was singularly attracted to one of these men, at first thinking it was because of his eccentric hat, but soon finding other things far more entertaining than this sombrero-like piece of millinery. He was gesticulating violently, in the manner of foreigners, but soon, with a slight shrug, he went out, bearing such a look of resignation on his face, that my first impulse was to go tell him how awfully sorry I was that things weren't going his way.

This was my first impression of Serge Oukrainsky. I know now that this was not exactly correct. Only once since then have I seen M. Oukrainsky really lose his temper, or forget his manners, and that is saying worlds for anyone in the theatrical profession. I have never known anyone so absolutely refined, with such high ideals, or so artistic. To look at his unusually high forehead, his deep, far-away eyes, his interesting paleness, one would think that he were surely a poet or a philosopher. Although he is neither of these in name, he seems to express the qualities of both in his dancing and designing. He never seems to be quite conscious of what is going on around him, perhaps it is only because he does not understand our language, but he gives the impression of always being a thousand miles away. It seems rather curious that a man of this temperament should take the comedian's parts, but he can be as ridiculously funny as he can be beautifully serious.

Anna Pavlova [1970]

The first time I ever saw Pavlova was in her dressing room, stark naked and picking her teeth. I have never seen such a perfect dancing body. She took a comb to my hair, parted it in the middle, and said, "This is for dancer."

Earth, air, fire, water—these were the elements of Pavlova's dancing. Underneath her delicate, fragile-looking body and her air of ethereality lurked such muscles of steel and such sensuous passion that no other dancer has rivaled her before or since. She cast her magic spell on one and all, and none who had ever seen her remained untouched. Her poetry and the deep melancholy of her Russian soul brought her audience invariably to tears. I weep myself even at the thought of her.

I was in her company for one year, on her last South American tour (1918-1919). My mother went with me, as my father and brother were in the army in France. I left school to go with Pavlova and went back to school when my father returned from the war. Mother became great friends with Pavlova, who often invited us to have tea with her. She gave me a beautiful Spanish shawl when I left the company.

(Inset left and right): Anna Pavlova, 1918, 1915. *(Above):* At Midway Gardens, 1915. *(Below):* The Pavlova Company in Lima, Peru, October 1918. Identifiable are Pavlova, Muriel Stuart, Ruth Page and Hilda Butsova.

To say that Pavlova was an inspiration is putting it mildly. For days after seeing her dance I felt as though I were walking on air. In the *Faust* ballet I was one of her slaves, and when I had the good luck to dance with her all alone across the entire stage I nearly fainted at the touch of her hand. I can feel her electric touch even now.

While I was in the company she never once gave the company class, nor did she seem particularly interested in the company. Almost everyone was attractive and most of them danced well. The girls were called the "Pavlovitas," and whenever we went out we were followed and stared at. Some man in Lima, Peru, sent me white roses every day. When we left he sent a box of candy to the boat. I opened it a week later and inside was a diamond and sapphire necklace! My mother made me send it right back. I never even *met* the man!

I later joined the Diaghileff company, and now I can clearly see the difference between the two companies and *why* Pavlova danced only one season with Diaghileff. I think he might have called a number of her divertissements candy-box art (for example her very popular *Gavotte* danced to the "Glowworm" music), while Diaghileff's aim was always to create something new and startling, something that was really art, with dancing sometimes quite incidental. Diaghileff discovered exciting young composers, artists, dancers, and choreographers; Pavlova was content to use pretty tunes of the past and conventional costumes. Diaghileff had a whole company of stars (repressed); in *her* company, Pavlova was the one and only, incomparable to the end.

Seven Poems [1928-1929]

[These poems, reflecting the influence of a broad literary background yet bearing their own sensual, rhythmic quality, were written when Ruth Page was returning to the United States from Japan via Southeast Asia, the Middle East, and Europe, after having performed at the coronation ceremonies of Emperor Hirohito in October 1928. Only seven out of many more poems found in a small notebook kept by Miss Page are printed here.]

(Above): Ruth Page at the Taj Mahal, 1928-9. (Below): Ruth Page in India, 1928-9.

(Left): Ruth Page at Djakarta, 1929. *(Right):* Ruth Page at the Taj Mahal, 1929.

1

The Flapper's Philosophy

I am the essence of the wind-blown bob,
I'm the modern girl, pert and snappy;
None of this romantic stuff for me,
I take my men where I find them,
And I find them—pretty swell;
Love is just sex for me.

My legs are damnably pretty
I know it and therefore I like to swim;
My parents think I'm kind of rotten
But say, parents mean pocket-books
And nothing more to me.

I take my jazz fast and furious,
None of this nature dancing for me,
It's the bunk and they know it
So bother them, and come with me, boys.
I'll show you a time—I'm like the jazz,
Red hot, fast, and terribly free.   Java

2

A tawny young lad from the west was my lover,
And naught of love did he know,
Till we met one night at the Lido,
And he felt and I felt all different,
From aught we had felt before.
That night at the Lido was rapturous,
Like a dream it floated by.
In the morning, I said,
"What are you doing here?"
And he smiled, "I'm a tourist, my dear,
Good-bye!"   Pnom-Penh

3

New York, my dream, my love,
You seem so white, so towering—
Cubical against the blue.
By night you flash so dizzily
By day you dance so glowingly,
You are the fountain of eternal youth
Utterly mad in the turmoil of your success.
Your lovers all tire of you, yes,
But your lovers all return to you,
Great dazzling city
Modern with the beauty of the new world,
With no thoughts of the old world,
But reaching high,
Up beyond your fairy roof gardens
Luring the Greek, the Roman,
And all the world,
With your joy, with your riches,
With your vibrant living.
New York, my dream, my first love,
I come back to you
Fresh from foreign lands
To lay my heart again
At your . . . feet.   *Homeric*, April 3 [1929]

4

Come to me
As you would come
To some cool spring
In Summer.
Dip your hands
Into the snowy clusters
Of my hidden thoughts
And take from me
The Strength
To stare at the great stars of night—
To tread the bare earth by day—
In silence and alone.

Come to me
As you would come
To some red fire
In Winter.
Dip your hands
Into the burning recesses
Of my throbbing brain
And take from me
The Power
to face the black abysses of midnight—
To stride the bleak skies by noon—
In sorrow and in death.

Come to me
In winter and in springtime
In sadness and in joy
And dip your hands
Into the deep still fountain
Of my love.

5

I walked in the footsteps of my childhood
With the phantom of my lover who was gone.
The sad wind swept through the pine trees
Wooingly whispering of nights remembered
On hilltops, when two bodies swayed as one—
Swayed as in the dance of Siva
Who danced on top of the world
And remained alone triumphant
Viewing the earth and himself from afar.
We thought of heaven—
And found that mystic union
In the rhythm of our bodies
On the hilltops
Of those far-off childish days.

6

I waited till the tall grass
Sickened and sighed—
I waited till the night owls
Hooted and cried—
I waited till my soul paled,
Shivered and died.

Love should be light, love should be trite,
Love should last only one night.
What isn't bright, cannot be right,
Love for me has lost all its bite.

Bitter night when song is not,
Bitter day with music fled,
Love is just a lot of rot,
Who is worth a tear to shed?

Now let's be through with weeping
For the world is mad and gay
And now I feel like sweeping
All the old loves far away.

7

I bring to you with my hands
Gleanings from the large world.
I bring to you with my feet
Rhythms of distant lands.
My eyes are black, big with the mystery of rain-clouds
Hanging shadowy over fearsome craters;
Brilliant with gazing too steadily into burning suns,
Into lovers' eyes, drowned with dewiness
On starlit nights.
I bring to you holy thoughts of India
Spiritual home of mad desires
To enter into nothingness, to leave the flesh
All rotting, and be transported beyond
This ravishing earth.
With my breasts I bring to you all the joy of fleeting happiness
Of sudden longing, despair to catch at beauty
To hold it ever in your dream's eye.
All this I bring to you, and even more
For my soul has been journeying
Deep into the heart of this bright sad world.

Java

PART II.

Dancing Around the World

My Side of the Footlights: An American Ballerina Analyzes and Compares Dance Audiences on Three Continents

[In *The Dance*, June 1926]

The most stimulating experience in any dancer's life, I think, is to dance within the period of a few months in places as widely separated in distance and artistic expression as Monte Carlo, Buenos Aires, and Chicago. Within the past year I have had the good fortune to dance in each of them and to observe dancing and dancers in Europe, North America, and South America—ballet dancers, folk dancers, ballroom dancers, some of them brilliant, some stupid, some mediocre, but all invariably stimulating. And the more I see of dancing the more absorbing and fascinating it becomes—full of thrills, disappointments, but always full of interest. Each country has something to offer, each experience has something to add, to the growth of the dancer as an artist.

In Paris, dancing as a whole is surprisingly mediocre. The opera ballet is dull and old-fashioned, as if the spark of artistic life had died out of it long ago or been overwhelmed by rigid conventions of French tradition, and the dancing in the revues and vaudeville can only be called stupid. Perhaps the latter is the more surprising, for it seems curious that the French producer before a French audience, especially in Paris, which the world knows as the center of art and fashion, should show such little taste in putting on what we Americans call a "show." At the moment, the French producer seems to rely exclusively on the light and witty dialogue of his comedians and the gorgeous effects of costume and scenery to make his production a success; but the dancing, while very pretentious, fails to satisfy because of its essential vulgarity. Whether this is simply because the dancers do not know how to dance or because the public does not demand first-class dancing as part of its light entertainment, I do not know, but nothing could be less artistic and more unattractive than the untrained dancers in their scanty costumes on the French stage generally today. Any first-class American chorus girl becomes a prima ballerina by comparison.

In mentioning the American chorus girl in connection with the Paris revues, one should not forget to state that many of them are in fact appearing in Paris at the present time and have had the greatest success. The Gertrude Hoffmann girls are the

(Above): Front curtain for Chicago Allied Arts by Nicholas Remisoff, Ruth Page, premiere danseuse, at center. *(Below):* Ruth Page in *The Rivals,* 1926. Photo by G. Maillard Kessiere.
(Right): Ruth Page in *Le Coq d'Or,* 1925. Photo by Bixio y Castiglioni.

Chicago Allied Arts production of *Mandragora,* 1926. Ruth Page is standing on right.
Photo by Underwood.

talk of Europe because of their freshness and virility and their highly trained acrobatic and jazz dancing—and, of course, there are also the Tiller girls from England. However, I intended to speak rather of the artistic dancing which, as I have said, simply does not exist on the lighter French stage today.

Nevertheless, France, and particularly its little principality on the Côte d'Azur, still harbors and contributes largely to the support of Diaghileff's Russian Ballet, the greatest dancing institution in the world for the last fifteen years or more, which for some time past has been more or less permanently situated in Monte Carlo, where it is supported by the princess of Monaco. In spite of brief visits each season to Spain and Paris and a somewhat longer stay in London each year, the ballet has come to regard Monte Carlo as its home and the famous Casino as its domicile. One is continually hearing the remark that the Russian ballet is not what it once was. Perhaps this is true, but to one who has never seen it in its earlier days, it is still glorious. Diaghileff, with his peculiar genius for surrounding himself with talented artists in every art, seems incapable of doing anything which in some respect at least is not well worth while.

The new ballets of Massine, Nijinska, and Balanchine, even if they are not always completely satisfying, are invariably original, usually delightful, often very clever. Perhaps Diaghileff's greatest success at present, as it appears to be his greatest interest, is with painting as it is associated with the stage. I was greatly impressed with the fiery and austere intensity of Picasso, with Marie Laurencin's delicious pink and French-blue femininity, both in such tremendous contrast to the mass and colors of Bakst's overwhelming Oriental creations.

It seems to me that most of the newer ballets are in a much lighter vein than the old Fokine and Nijinsky ballets, but this is in the spirit of the age. Perhaps it is the effect of the war and of too much seriousness. At any rate, the new ballets seem more expressive of our own generation; they are clever rather than beautiful; the age of the athletic girl and boy. At the same time and in pleasing contrast, Diaghileff has revived a number of very old classical ballets, and it seems strange, among the rococo surroundings of the Casino, to see a Diaghileff ballerina in short tarleton skirts dancing the old-fashioned pas de deux and pas seuls of the *Lac des Cygnes.*

Unfortunately, Diaghileff has no very unusually talented dancers at present, although most are excellent. Many of his dancers have been in the company for more than ten years, which gives him the great advantage of knowing his material and its limitations thoroughly. In addition, he has not to worry about the ensemble which the long years of training have made almost perfect. Of the principals, Dolin, the Irishman, has been very successful this year and Tchernicheva, Sokolova (who, in spite of her Russian name, as all Europe knows is thoroughly English), Nemchinova, and Woizikowsky are always first-class artists.

Balanchine, a young Russian boy barely twenty years of age, is the most interesting of the new choreographers; he lacks the experience, of course, and unquestionably also the extraordinary cleverness of Massine, but he nevertheless gives promise of something very unusual. He has the great advantage of having been trained as a musician in Russia in the Imperial schools and seems thoroughly imbued with the spirit of modern music.

Of the present-day composers, Stravinsky still reigns supreme, although Auric, Dukelsky, and Poulenc have added interesting and attractive ballets to Diaghileff's repertoire. I was personally somewhat less impressed with Milhaud, although in *Le Train Bleu* he had certainly accomplished what he set out to do—to be banal—and the ballet had quite a popular success. Poulenc's charming tunes get into one's blood much as Irving Berlin's latest jazz melodies do. Auric is more subtle; his *Les Matelots* was a success of the past spring and summer; and Dukelsky has talent which may some day produce great work. It is, in fact, Diaghileff's gift to discern talent in artists who have neither developed nor become known, and this may be some day regarded as his greatest contribution to modern art.

One should not speak of the Russian ballet without devoting a special paragraph to Maestro Enrico Cecchetti, the great Italian teacher of classic ballet. He is now too old to travel with the Diaghileff Ballet, but he always joins them for the season at Monte Carlo. Monte Carlo is not far from his home in Italy, and Maestro enjoys returning to his old pupils again with the warm Riviera sunshine. Whenever Diagheliff is particularly interested in a dancer he insists upon Cecchetti lessons, and every morning at nine o'clock the entire company must come to his class in the Salle des Repétitions in one wing of the Casino, no matter how late the performance has lasted the night before—and in Europe they usually last very late. Cecchetti, in spite of his seventy-eight years, teaches with great vigor the strictest Italian technique, which as most of us agree is the best foundation for every kind of dancing.

The most interesting thing about Cecchetti's teaching is that he has well-thought-out theories, the result of his long years of association with the dance, and he puts them into practice with a vengeance. The impression that stands out most clearly in the minds of his pupils is his particular emphasis on the correct positions of the arms and head, concerning which he has written so much in his books on the dance. It is this perfect harmony of the head and arms with the rest of the body which gives the Cecchetti pupils what the artist calls "finish." I think our American dancers have more vitality and perhaps more personality than most of the European dancers, but we so often lack this thing called finish which is so characteristic of the European artist. We are always in too great a hurry to get into the details and intricacies of our art, and what is worse, the teachers in this country are always in a hurry too. Unfortunately for us, we have no Cecchetti in America constantly to bring us back to our ideal. The true measure of any teacher is his pupils. Pavlova, Karsavina, Bolm, Nijinsky, Massine, and Lopokova—in fact, most of the great dancers of the last fifty years—are all Cecchetti pupils; and though they may no longer adhere to the strictness of his techniques, they have all been trained in it as the foundation from which their success has come.

Everyone who knows him loves Cecchetti. The strictest and most terrifying person during his lessons, he will converse by the hour after them, and delights in telling amusing tales of all the famous dancers he has taught. Then Mme. Cecchetti, who is also an excellent teacher and an accomplished mime, helps him on with his coat and the pupils say good-bye each day with many kisses, to his invariable remark, that if we remember half of what he has taught us, we shall be doing well. It is a delight to know that Cecchetti this year has been granted the greatest honor within the power of his beloved Italy to bestow upon him, the position of Ballet Master at La Scala, the national theatre in Milan.

II

To go from dancing in Monte Carlo to dancing in Buenos Aires is a big jump not only geographically but artistically. The change is complete. Instead of a vital interest and desire for new experiments in all the arts that go to make up dancing, we have reached a city where the composers are mediocre, where the painters with the single exception of Fiagre are characterless, where Rimsky-Korsakov's *Coq d'Or* is considered ultra-modern, Debussy still novel, and the dancers are unrhythmical and scarcely know the simplest steps.

Yet Buenos Aires has its own tremendous possibilities. The Colon Opera House, if not the largest, is certainly one of the most beautiful theatres in the world; it has the true distinction of simplicity, gives the feeling of great space, and at the same time possesses a certain warmth and color which makes it most attractive and luxurious. Above all, however, I like the feeling of space here; one never feels cramped. Like so many other theatres, it has been built with comfort of the audience rather than the artist in mind. The lighting equipment is very old-fashioned, and the rehearsal room used by the ballet is like a dungeon.

With these difficulties, to which must be added that of the wholly untrained ballet, Adolph Bolm has produced the great opera-ballet *Coq d'Or* and Stravinsky's *Petrushka*. He also produced some of the dances from his own Ballet Intime. The results were astonishingly successful, and Buenos Aires was most responsive. We gave eight performances of *Coq d'Or* and seven of *Petrushka* during the season from June to September, whereas the most popular opera, which was *Aida*, was given only five times. *Lorelei*, the opera chosen for the gala performance for the Prince of Wales, had only three performances; and several of the other operas, such as *Cena della Beffe* and *Phedra*, had only two. For the first time in its history the Colon Opera was supported this year by the municipality of Buenos Aires; and, as is true in most opera companies, it was run at a great loss, which was rendered greater by the fact that practically all the artists came from Europe and North America. If in addition to the expense of traveling such great distances one considers the time and the money spent on each opera and the few performances given, the loss does not seem so surprising.

The Argentines have a habit of coming to the theatre very late, with the result that most theatres are half empty until after ten o'clock. As a consequence, the cinemas and the revues have been adjusted to the life of the people and are given in sections, beginning at nine and again at ten and eleven o'clock, the feature picture in a cinema and the best portion of the revue being generally shown at eleven o'clock or even as late as twelve o'clock. But for the opera which attempts to be an artistic whole, the custom is disastrous besides being very discourteous to the singers. However, once one is used to it, one comes to enjoy eating dinner with the Argentines at eight-thirty or nine o'clock and then spending no more than an hour in light entertainment at the theatre.

The audiences in Buenos Aires with the single exception of those at the Colon Theatre, which is the fashionable place for women to be seen, are striking because they are composed almost entirely of men. It is not considered proper for nice women to walk on the streets or to eat in restaurants, go to revues, or in fact appear in any way publicly. As one might expect, it is the men who frequent the cabarets, while their wives remain at home. Foreign women who do not live in Buenos Aires frequently go to the cabarets out of pure curiosity, but they are provided for in small private boxes on a balcony, where a lattice work permits them to look out but prevents those outside from looking in.

One notices everywhere in Buenos Aires the customs and manners of the French. Exactly as in the cafés on Montmartre, the visitor at Tabaris, which is the most attractive cabaret in Buenos Aires, instead of paying an entrance fee is expected to order a bottle of champagne immediately upon sitting down at the table, an unfamiliar custom to a North American.

The tango music forms the great attraction of these dancing places. The orchestra usually plays several jazz pieces and then an equal number of tangos, the jazz with every available light turned on and the tangos with scarcely any light at all. This lighting expresses the attitude of the people toward the music. The tangos are fascinatingly sad and are played extremely slowly in a manner quite unknown to any other city. The Argentine tango is danced quite simply without any fancy steps whatever, but of all ballroom dances I think it is the most dignified and the most beautiful. So slow and quiet and seductive does it seem, that one can dance it for hours without becoming tired. Not only is the music of the tango itself invariably sad, but the words of the accompanying songs are always about the lover whose sweetheart has deserted him or the sweetheart who has lost her lover. One cannot imagine an attempt to make them happy or gay. In fact, all Argentine music has the same characteristic; all their beautiful songs for the guitar are sweetly and romantically mournful.

The Argentine country dances are delightful and in *Juan Moreira* and *Julian Gininez*, two Argentine cowboy plays, we saw some of the picturesque Gaucho dances: the Pericon, danced usually by couples gracefully waving handkerchiefs; the Sombrerito, a dance with hats as the name implies; the Gato, an amusing dance founded on the actions of a cat, in which the partners pretend to hide from each other; and most fascinating of all, the Cuando, as noble and stately a dance as was ever seen in any court. The feeling in both music and steps of these country dances is undeniably Spanish, though the Argentine has added to it a distinctive character of his own. Fortunately, due partly to the efforts of Anna Cabrera, the Argentines are making a sincere effort to preserve and to develop their national art. She has had motion pictures taken of all the aspects of the life of the Indians and Gauchos, or cowboys, and has herself learned to play the guitar and sing their songs. She has even collected a company of native dancers who can now be seen in Buenos Aires itself. Her lecture and concert, which is an attempt to interpret the peasant art of the country, is one of the most interesting things in Buenos Aires.

III

Again a big jump, this time to Chicago, and one has reached a city as strikingly different from Monte Carlo and Buenos Aires as they are different from each other. No city has greater civic pride, and this is especially true of the support given to its artistic institutions.

Among the newest of these is the so-called Chicago Allied Arts, an organization composed of a group of people primarily interested in the modern arts related to music and the dance. It is their particular purpose to give Chicago a permanent and growing ballet commensurate with the expense and limitations of a small orchestra and devoted almost entirely to the production of works of living composers of every country.

The work of the organization is really founded upon a committee of artists composed of Adolph Bolm, Eric DeLamarter, and Nicholas Remisoff, under the directorship of John Alden Carpenter, all names well known to the musical and artistic world of this country.

Last year a ballet founded on an ancient Chinese legend dating from the sixth century, by Henry Eichheim, danced in authentic Chinese costumes; a *Little Circus*, the decor for which reminded one of the famous Cirque d'Hiver in Paris, to music by Offenbach; and a modern de Falla ballet called *El Amor Brujo* were among the new and successful works presented under the direction of the Chicago Allied Arts.

For the current season Mme. Herscher Clement has written a new and interesting French ballet laid in Paris, under the title *La Farce du Pont Neuf*. Karol Szymanowski, the most eminent living Polish composer, Arnold Schoenberg, from Austria, and Erik Satie, the French modernist composer, will each be represented by important works at one of the several groups of performances.

In commencing its second year the Chicago Allied Arts has been granted the immeasurable privilege of using the new Kenneth Sawyer Goodman Memorial Theatre, which forms a part of the Art Institute of Chicago on its famous Michigan Boulevard.

This theatre is used by the Chicago Allied Arts for its musical and dancing productions, as well as being a repertory theatre of the drama under the direction of the Art Institute. Not only does this connection bring the Chicago Allied Arts into intimate contact with the most popular of all museums of art, but the ballet in its turn will undoubtedly have an influence in keeping alive the spirit of modern art in the Art Institute itself.

One cannot but be hopeful after a review of the dancing in both Europe and South America that the greatest promise for the future seems to lie in our own country, in just such organizations as this ballet fostered by the Chicago Allied Arts.

A Balinese Rhapsody

[In *Theatre Arts Monthly*, November 1929]

We heard the music from the distance. It sounded like thousands of clear, tinkling bells, with every now and then a glorious mellow gong. Suddenly it became swift and mad. We ran breathlessly down the road, following the bells through the night. We came to a little temple, and there sat half the village, watching the dancing and listening to the music. Ordinarily it is the village dancing school in Bali which affords the entertainment; but every seventh night a more elaborate display is given in costume.

A slim boy starts the performance. He is dressed in a magenta and gold sarong, naked above the waist. His jaunty turban, of the same color as the skirt, is fashioned with a gold flower which trembles delicately when he moves. He sits in the center of the orchestra playing an instrument which appears, to a Westerner, much like a xylophone. He plays with arresting grace, brandishing his two sticks before striking the notes. These amusing embellishments suggest the tricks of a lively jazz drummer. The other musicians, sitting on the ground in the form of an open square, play upon handsomely carved, gilded instruments. The Balinese do not have written music. It seemed to me that they took a simple theme and devised extemporaneously every imaginable variation upon it, obtaining astonishingly rich orchestral effects.

Mario, the beautiful, magenta-clad youth, puts his sticks aside, picks up his fan, and begins a dance. It is one of the most esoteric dances I have ever seen. No verbal description can do more than hint at its meaning. He accomplishes the entire dance while sitting on the ground, with legs crossed underneath. He moves restlessly, flutters fingers back and forth, up and down, and makes intricate and unexpected angles with his fan. One is held by the strange expression of his face. The mouth is always closed, but sometimes an almost half-smile flickers on his lips as if he were amused by some secret—a little wicked, perhaps, but very sweet, his eyes half closed as if the better to recall and cherish the sweetness. Suddenly he opens his eyes very widely and fiercely. He frowns, and looks intently down, then up, then

A Balinese Rhapsody, dance by Ruth Page. Photo by Maurice Goldberg.

Ruth Page in Bali.

alluringly to one side. Now he glides over the ground with the smoothness of a snake coiling, and his eyes seem bright and curious like those of a wild animal in the jungle. Abruptly the music increases tempo; and then with the sounding of a soft, minor gong it becomes slow and seductive. In this mood the music accompanies the dance, which continues for about forty minutes. There is no climax at the end; the movement simply ceases. And there is no applause; no one understands applause in Bali.

After Mario's dance two little girls came into the center of the orchestra. They were dressed in the coventional *Legong* costume, which consists of a tight gold and green brocaded skirt, long sleeves, and strips of bright material wrapped tightly around the upper part of the body. They wore beautiful headdresses of filigreed leather, painted gold; and in the middle of their foreheads gleamed a tiny spot of white.

32

The *Legong* is a religious dance which the children begin to study when they are five years old. It requires three or four years to learn the *Legong*, and it is then performed for a few brief years only; for at the age of twelve or fourteen their religion compels them to give it up. These children are extremely serious; they never smile or open their mouths while dancing. The face remains quite calm, expressionless, except the eyes, which seem to move with rhythms utterly opposed to those of the head. In fact it is the head and eyes which complete the movements of the whole body. One thinks of the gestures of birds and snakes, or even horizontal swayings and revolvings of machinery. Yet all is stylized, of an apparent deep religious significance.

This side-to-side movement, so difficult for the human head and neck, must be accomplished without the slightest shifting of the shoulders. The hands and fingers have also their individual motions, like the vibrations of a serpent's tongue, or the trembling of petals, emphasized by the long fingernails of the left hand only. A fan is usually carried in the right hand, while the dancer moves the fingers of the left hand quickly from side to side, holding still the middle finger, the thumb, and the palm. The body shuffles and shakes, and bends, and twists unreasonably as if it felt a kind of ecstasy, while the features retain their trancelike immobility. Perhaps again, as in so much of Eastern culture, there is symbolized the ultimate conquest of the soul in its struggle with the body.

At last the youthful dancers sit calmly down as if nothing at all had happened. During a brief pause they are given tea; then, apparently refreshed, they start their exotic movements again. Each dance lasts from thirty to forty minutes. Not only are the dances physically difficult, but they are true feats of memory.

The next night there was no performance, but we went to the temple to watch the dancing lesson. There was the same crowd, the same enchanting orchestra, and the same two girls we had seen the night before. They were not in costume, but wore only their tight, long skirts, nothing above the waist. Their long, black hair was tied up with a towel into a knot at the side of the head. This night their two still younger pupils were working and it was a rare sight to watch the twelve-year-old girls teach the five-year-old babies. Their method of teaching is quite different from ours. The younger children follow the older ones and copy their movements precisely. If any mistake is made, the older girl steps behind her special charge and taking a firm hold of the child's arms, manipulates them for her through the entire dance until she sees the child is repeating it correctly. They never stop to review any step; they take the dance straight through from beginning to end, and they do this practically every night for three years until they know the motions of the different dances.

The children never laugh or play during their lessons, and even in the intermissions they sit quietly and calmly. Only once in a while is there a slight, childish smile, when someone has made a joke, for the Balinese are a jolly people and they love to laugh. The old maestro sits quietly with the orchestra, singing and watching the dancers intently. He seldom corrects them, as the older girls are supposed to be quite perfect by the time they are allowed to be models for the little ones. I found out later, however, that the presence of Eda Buda, the old maestro, was an extremely important incentive or influence. When he is not present, the children and even the older girls are inclined to dance indifferently; they are lazy, and their dance is quite another thing when the old master is not looking on. He himself is a fine dancer and a great pantomimist.

The next morning we saw the girls and boys of the village do what they call the "pleasure dance," so called because it is not religious. It is really a drama, and the stories are usually taken from the *Ramayana*. About thirty boys and girls performed the dance outside the temple walls, under a huge, spreading banyan tree. The setting is ideal, and although to me the dances are not as interesting as the *Legong*, they make a fascinating picture—the girls in their white and yellow flowered head dresses, bright and dazzling in the sunlight, and the village youths sitting in a circle, with fierce black mustaches and large red flowers stuck amusingly behind the ears. The movements are similar to those of the *Legong*, but done by the older girls, they seemed less precise and less dramatic. The girls develop so quickly in the tropics that after twelve they become much softer and rounder. Their dances seemed more arresting when performed with the harsh angularity of the children.

To me, all of Bali seemed like an orchid-haunted garden of dreams; sounds, flowers, people are soft and sweet. There is a delicious moment between consciousness and sleep in which a simple impression gathers about itself a strange and luminous logic—a moment in which apparent facts are seen and understood through a lens of magic atmosphere. When I recapture the twilight and look through it again, I am tempted to say of Bali that its music, people, and flowers are imbued with a single enchanting spirit which haunts them all. And though I can recall quite accurately the days of my enchantment in Bali, to me their reality is but the outward expression of my dream.

Through Propaganda to Art   [1930]

Spring blows fiercely into Moscow, while in the city's leading opera house the prima ballerina rides onto the stage sitting triumphantly on top of a tractor. And what have tractors to do with art and the theatre and spring in Moscow? The answer is that spring brings a special kind of seasonal propaganda to the city. It means a deliberate call to the open, after the indoor life of the long, stern Russian winter. The ballet is entitled *The Footballer*. And what have tractors to do with football? To be sure the hero of the ballet is a football player, but this is completely unimportant. *The Footballer* is just a title which is intended to convey a general idea of life out-of-doors, of young people going in strongly for sports, and the tractor is introduced at the end of the ballet as a symbol of Russia industrialized, a vision of a new Russia peopled with healthy young workers from the cities, with peasants making the country prosperous by means of the tractor.

Contrary to popular belief, the theatre in Moscow today is not an "art form" set apart from the life of the people. It is primarily a forum in which to educate the masses to Communistic ideals and ways of thinking. No other institution in Russia is more completely a part of the existing communal scheme. Audience, performers, productions—Communism has invaded them all. Frequently the play, opera, or ballet deals entirely with a revolutionary subject, but when it does not there is certain to be propaganda long before the last act is reached. As if to make up for any previous deficiency, the curtain goes down with red flags waving all over the stage, enormous pictures of Lenin floating down from the flies, and the audience applauding madly, if not for the play, then for the symbols of the national idealism.

The Footballer, which had its premiere on April 3, 1930, is a perfect prototype of the new, and it must be admitted, popular theatrical productions of the Russian capital. In the spring of the preceding year there had been no propaganda of sport in Moscow, nor indeed, elsewhere in Russia. Neither the nudist cults of nearby Germany nor the more frankly unconventional forms of the dance inspired by such artist as Wigman and Laban had leapt that extraordinary barrier which artificially cuts

35

Ruth Page in Moscow, 1930.

Russia off from Western Europe. But the powers that be had decided that sport must come to the people. The opening performance had been accurately timed to coincide with the first break in the long Russian winter and the first signs of the late Russian spring.

The first act of *The Footballer* is largely devoted to the joy of sport. A handsome young football player jumps over a high brick wall over which his ball has just fallen, onto the stage. It is quite the same introduction as in the *Jeux* of Debussy and Nijinsky, with the scene changed from tennis to football. There he finds an attractive young girl sweeping leaves. She is dressed in a middy blouse and short skirt, and wears tan tights and toe shoes. Her skin is sun-tanned, her hair bobbed. They dance a pas de deux. The toe shoes and the classical adagio are in marked contrast with the modern spirit of football player, girl and football. However, the dance was so well done, its spirit so completely athletic, in spite of the toe shoes and the conventional ballet movements, that one soon forgot any incongruities of style. Quite evidently the footballer and the girl fall in love, but the story of their adventures is rather lost in the maze of dances which follow.

The scene shifts. The whole corps de ballet appears in sport clothes and runs in single file across the front of the stage while bright lights move very rapidly in the opposite direction on the backdrop, giving the whole spectacle an illusion of great speed and brilliance. The scene following is "in one." A girl and six men dance in the style of our own musical comedies, though they greatly exaggerate our modern type of ballroom dancing. As no Russians are permitted to dance American ballroom jazz dances in Moscow today, the purpose behind this caricature is unmistakable. The scene shifts again to disclose a tennis game danced by two men and two girls. Their movements are likewise in the classical style. The act ends with an exciting rugby football game which gives the impression of a real football scrimmage without being in the least realistic.

The first act of *The Footballer* just described is by far the strongest of the three long acts. The idea of sport was interestingly carried out and the action moved with great vitality and speed. If not great art, the ballet is nevertheless an excellent show and its success as propaganda must be great. To an American who had never seen a single ballet in an opera house continue for three hours the experience was quite novel. The Russians have no musical comedies or revues in the American sense, although the Blue Blouse, a theatrical organization which goes about to workmen's clubs, provides a kind of vaudeville. Their place, however, is taken by these long ballets. They are for the most part light, both musically and artistically, and the dancing is so excellent and varied that the audience is continually entertained.

The second set of *The Footballer* takes place in an amusement park. There is much clever modern dancing in it, but the story becomes rather confused and there is so much chasing about and leaping and throwing things around that one is reminded of our own early movie comedies. In the third act the football hero and the girl are reunited by a group of children, each of whom brings in a large red letter. The children group themselves at the back, the letters spelling in Russian, "All to the Carnival," which serves to introduce a long series of divertisements, most of the dances pointing some moral or teaching some lesson. The men perform a very striking dance composed mostly of Swedish setting-up exercises; they are joined by the girls who show the girls' method of exercising. Then follow a series of dances depicting electricity, fire and water, interpreted in old fashioned classical style, the only important one being that danced by the famous new dancer, Messerer, in which he does magnificent leaps, entrechat six, and pirouettes, the like of which I have never seen. The Russians do not seek to impress one with a technique of acrobatic stunts, but by the sheer beauty and perfection with which the simpler steps are executed. The Bolshoi Opera school has developed amazing dancers, both in technique and dramatic expression. As far as I could discover, the school itself is unchanged in spite of all the upheavals of government.

After Messerer's solo came the dance of the veiled oriental girl. She is accompanied by a dreadful old man who mistreats her, from whom she is of course rescued by a dashing young Communist who tears off her veil and her long dresses and dances with her a dance of victory. The Russian peasants then offer a harvest dance, and it is after this dance that Abramova, the premiere danseuse, comes riding in on the tractor to symbolize the development of Russian farming and the progress of the peasant. The curtain goes down upon a spectacular but conventional tableau. One's impression is of an effort to accomplish something new in the theatre but with the old means shot through with an all-pervading propaganda.

The Red Poppy is another three act ballet done in the pre-revolutionary manner. It has had an unusual success, having already been given two hundred and ten times in Moscow, but to me it was much less interesting than *The Footballer.* Though using a Chinese setting, a great part of the ballet is done on the toes, and in spite of amazingly fine dancing, I would have preferred it had it been frankly classical. The music was pleasant enough but very light and not at all unusual.

I had heard before going to Russia that very few of the old operas were given and that those which were had been distorted to suit the Communists, but I did not find this true. The Bolshoi Opera has a very large repertoire of operas and ballets, old and new. I saw both *Prince Igor* and *Sadko* in one week, neither of which had been changed in any way. The change is in the audience. In the beautiful old theatre one now sees only working people dressed in working clothes, although at the premiere of *The Footballer* there were a few evening dresses. The theatres are always full and one usually sees a good many children, particularly at the Bolshoi Opera. They seem to give as many of the Russian operas as possible. In these I was disappointed to find that the ballets are completely conventional opera ballets. The most interesting opera which I saw was a new opera in the small opera house called *Proreev,* or *Driving Through,* with music by Pototzkov and decors by Youdeen. The music was very Russian in spirit and the story dealt with the civil war in Russia after the revolution. The sets were constructivist and whenever the story required a larger scenic panorama than the stage itself would permit, they lowered a movie screen and continued the action there. Most of the fighting between the Red and White Armies was done on the screen, and there were many scenes showing the peasants with the landowners; and in one instance the dramatic escape of a young peasant boy from the Cossack army.

One of the most interesting scenes on the stage was in the home of one of the White officers. A group of officers are sitting around drinking. Gradually the party gets gayer and gayer. The men dance with each other, burlesquing the ballet dancers and the peasants, until they become so excited that they finally end up by sitting astride their chairs and galloping about the room. The scene was cleverly staged and very funny but we were the only people in the audience laughing. I asked my Russian friend why the audience did not laugh and she said that this scene was given only to show how disgustingly the officers of the White Army behaved and that it was, therefore, nothing to laugh at. I noticed that in other plays and operas which I saw the bourgeoisie were usually depicted as drinking and having extravagant parties. There were beautiful peasant songs and dances in *Proreev.* In the last act the peasants and proletarians sing together while the peasant boy hero tells of his escape from the Cossacks. This is followed by an attack by the Whites, and it is a very dramatic moment when the soldiers run over and under the bridge and up and down the constructivist set with flashlights playing on them from above. The final victory of the Reds—the triumphant red flag and the enormous picture of Lenin filling half the stage—was, one felt, modern Russia at its Reddest.

One of my first performances in Moscow was in a church which had been rebuilt into a workmen's club. The workmen's clubs of Moscow are fulfilling a great need of the people, where housing conditions are and always have been bad. Nightly at any club you will find large groups of working people reading or playing games and enjoying the concerts and performances especially arranged for them. Over two hundred concerts a month are given in Moscow and everything that is given is strictly censored. No vulgar entertainment is permitted, no suggestive costumes may be worn, only the best music can be played, and the performances must be largely propagandistic or educational. All the artists in Moscow are working and, while they do not receive large salaries, at least they are all sure of work.

It is the religious situation which foreigners seem to think is the worst feature of the Communist regime. But when one is actually in Moscow one feels that the religious situation is much healthier and more normal than is, for instance, the religious situation in Spain. In Spain the poor people give their last pennies to contribute to the richness of the Virgin's robe worn at the Easter parade. The effect in the parade is sometimes very lovely and certainly very theatrical. Probably the people are deeply moved by the religious significance of the Virgin's effigy, but one cannot help feeling that the money would be better spent if it were used to educate the superstitious and ignorant. In Moscow any older persons who care to go to church may go and it is completely untrue that there are no church services held in the old manner. As many churches are available as there are older people to fill them. It is those that remain which are made into museums or used as workingmen's clubs. As everyone knows, religion is not encouraged, and the children are brought up entirely in the religion of Communism in which, of course, the old church does not exist.

The Russians go to extremes in many instances. While they are very anxious to educate the people they would not tell the audience, in explaining my Balinese dances, that these are ancient religious dances. It surprised me that, close as Russia is to the Orient, they know very little about oriental dancing and my Balinese dances were a great surprise to them. One of the favorite themes of dance Communist propaganda is the veiled oriental girl saved by the Communists, already referred to. Of course the theme is dramatic material which is used over and over again. It appeared in a performance especially given for me at the studio of Tschernitskaia. In this version the heroine of the occasion was a Communist girl scout and the scene took place somewhere in the Caucaucus. As usual, the men were mistreating the women and the girl scout had to give the oriental woman courage to break away. The Tschernitskaia studio dancers gave a large variety of dances, some in the old classical style which Tschernitskaia still considers the best foundation for dance artists, some in modern German technique, and a number of delightful Russian peasant dances. In these the dancers make cries very much like those of the Spanish gypsies in Granada. Fortunately the present government is doing everything to preserve Russian peasant art and one can see peasant dances and hear peasant songs in almost any theatre in Moscow. The Blue Blouse association, with its vaudeville-like show, gives many peasant dances and songs and they do them in real peasant style. At the Bolshoi Opera the peasant songs and dances are also amazingly well done and the funny antics of the peasant clowns in *Sadko* are something never to be forgotten. There is a large store run by the government devoted entirely to peasant products where one may buy Russian dolls, linens, and all kinds of Russian toys.

Social jazz dancing is frowned upon in Moscow and one sees very few Russians at the Grand Hotel where the foreigners go to dance. Miss Tschernitskaia gave in one of her compositions a very graphic description of how the Communists feel towards modern ballroom dancing. Two girls in brown tights do a monkey dance. Another girl in modern dress, enters and does a jazz dance. After she dances, the two monkeys pull off her skirt and immediately she changes her expression and also becomes monkey-like in appearance. The three monkeys contrive a caricature of modern ballroom dancing. Then to show a striking contrast, four girl scouts do a virile dance based on modern athletic movements and old Russian peasant dances. Always a moral in Russia.

The dancing school connected with the Bolshoi Opera is one of the many anachronisms of present-day Moscow. From all the descriptions I have heard of it as it existed under the Czars, from Pavlova, Bolm, and numerous Russian dancers, I think it has changed very little since the Revolution. The Metropolitan Opera ballet of New York considers itself lucky to have two large studios. The Chicago Opera ballet has one medium size studio. But in Moscow, where four or five people are accustomed to live in one room, the ballet school has some eight studios, four of which are unusually large. I watched classes in fencing and in all types of dancing, beginning with very young children and proceeding to special classes for the girls, special classes for the boys, and special classes for the six principal dancers. Children take an active part in the opera performances. There is almost no ballet where the children do not appear, so that they become used to the stage at a very early age. After seeing the children of the ballet school, it is easy to understand why Isadora Duncan adored the Russian children. They are completely natural and spontaneous. One does not need to dance special children's dances for them. They watched all my dances attentively and appreciatively. After the performance they all shouted and came up and threw their arms around me and kissed me.

Although I did not see Mme. Geltzer I understand that she is still the premiere danseuse par excellence, in spite of her sixty years. One afternoon I gave a special performance for the artists of the school and I found them even more unusual as an audience than the workmen for whom I had danced the night before. After finishing the program and having already repeated some of the numbers, I had to go back to the beginning and start the program all over again. I told them about our American composer, Gershwin, and they were particularly interested in my interpretation of his *Preludes*. They asked to have the music left with them so that they could copy it and try some of the dances themselves. Most Europeans do not quite understand the mood of our "blues" and even of our ordinary jazz, but I believe that the Russians do so more than the others. After the performance a tea was arranged and I met the artists. They were, of course, most interested in hearing about all of the Russian dancers in America, and I, on the other hand, was most eager to hear about the new Russian dancers in Russia and what they were planning to do. Unfortunately there was no time to visit the Duncan school but I saw them give a performance in one of the cinema theatres, and their revolutionary dances seemed completely in line with all the progaganda of which I had already seen so much in the other theatres. I think it would have been impossible for Isadora not to have created those dances after coming to Russia.

One feels on leaving Russia that one would like a little more art for art's sake. On the other hand, the Russian passion for propaganda lends a distinctiveness to the theatre and to Russian art in general which is certainly unique. Revolutionary subjects are invariably stimulating to the creative artist, and one feels the same kind of fanaticism and faith in the art of Communistic Russia that one feels, for instance, behind the paintings of an El Greco. Communism is now a religion in Russia even if they do not like to call it by that name.

With such a background of revolutionary thinking and with such a predominance of Red, it is rather paradoxical that Russian art is still at heart very classical. I heard no composer in Moscow as "modern" even as Prokofieff, and in fact some of Prokofieff's metallic but thrilling compositions seem more expressive of contemporary Russia than the music that is being composed in Moscow today. In Prokofieff's music there is a sternness, a brilliance and a clearness of thought that seems quite definitely to crystallize something in the air of Moscow today. I can imagine the people moving forward fearlessly, inspired by the music of a Prokofieff march.

Even the music for *Proreev,* the most revolutionary theatrical piece which I have seen, was at heart classical, as was also the music of *The Footballer.* The dancers are doing some new things and doing them well, but their classical dancing is still, I believe, their unique gift to the world.

The Dances of Japan: Seen Through the Eyes of an Occidental Artist

[In *Musical America*, November 10, 1934]

Returning to Tokyo after an absence of six years, I was amazed at the great changes that have taken place theatrically in the third largest city in the world. My first impressions of Tokyo were gained when I went there in 1928 to dance in the Imperial Theatre for performances in honor of the enthronement celebrations of Emperor Hirohito. The beautiful modern Imperial Theatre, which was at that time under the

(Above): Harald Kreutzberg, A. Strok, Ruth Page and Friedrich Wilckens in Japan, 1934.
(Below): With Mitsugoro Bando, 1934.

expert direction of E. Yamamoto and was giving superb drama both ancient and modern, is now a motion picture palace. This is a symbol of what has taken place theatrically in Japan during the period of depression.

The Japanese motion picture syndicate headed by Mr. Otani and known as the Shochiku Trust now owns or controls more than 300 theatres of every kind, Kabuki, doll, geisha, Noh, Bugaku, as well as picture houses, throughout the empire and controls through long-term contracts the majority of its leading actors, singers, and dancers.

Under its former management the Imperial Theatre not only supported a permanent repertory company (a large group of actors, actresses, musicians, artists, and dancers of the highest standard) qualified to produce any form of Japanese drama, but it made possible the appearances in Tokyo of eminent European and American artists.

The theatre was equipped to produce Noh plays in the strictest Japanese classical style. But more important than this, the company experimented, building a new style, modern in feeling, but growing logically out of Japanese theatrical tradition. For the first time men and women played together. Amazing as are the onagatas (men who take women's parts), the time has certainly come when Japanese women should take a place for themselves in the Japanese theatre. Excellent actresses, indeed, were those whom I saw in the Imperial Theatre plays. Particularly impressive was Miss Mori, who appeared in an unforgettable drama entitled *Love-crazed*. For over an hour she acted, sang, and danced, assisted by choruses and excellent lighting effects. This was not a drama of objective plot and action but a study of the psychological state of a woman demented from love. It was perhaps rather a dance interwoven with words than a play enhanced with dance, so perfectly were the varied elements synchronized.

Madness from love seems to be a favorite subject in the Japanese theatre. This year at the Kabuki-za we saw Kikugoro Onoye in one of the old Kabuki dramas, perform a solo dance (with words) in which he depicted a lovelorn youth. He danced with the kimono of his love, the expressive emptiness of his beloved's garment and the strange wail in his unnatural voice disclosing a dance drama of tragic beauty. Sometimes long and tedious to a Westerner, these solo dances nevertheless are deeply impressive. One never forgets the idea, the picture, the slow movement. In comparison, our solo dances, usually lasting three to five minutes, seem of fleeting beauty. For our impatient American audiences we hit the high spots, so to speak. The audience may applaud wildly, but desires to proceed immediately to further excitement. The Japanese dancer seems to sink into the collective consciousness of his undemonstrative public. The same dances are repeated generation after generation, with the result that the personality of the dancer is absorbed in the content of the thought. The ideas and the movements are repeated endlessly; the dance has crystallized into the completeness of a finished work of art, the past speaking to the present, and the present absorbed in eternal values.

In 1928 I saw Osani's Little Theatre, which was modern in the same sense as our little theatre movement; but since his death no one has been able to carry on his excellent work. Now one sees movies and revues, both American and Japanese. The Japanese revue is a hybrid of East and West. The Japanese imitate all the worst features of our shows and have none of the essential brilliance and racy spirit so typical of our Broadway Jewish and Negro Americanism.

Tap dancing and toe dancing seem to have an irresistible appeal for the Japanese—but these dance forms are unsuited to the Japanese physique. At the Geisha Theatre in Kyoto I was fortunate enough to see the spring celebrations, and at the beginning of the program was completely captivated with the rows of exquisite girl singers and samisen players on either side of the theater, and with the doll-like geishas in their elaborate costumes performing their refined dances. Suddenly all this loveliness and delicacy disappeared, to be followed by the most banal scenes, copies from the cheapest type of American revue. But the English program notes have an unwitting humor all their own.

If, however, Japanese modernism seems to have run amuck, the old Kabuki Theatre still maintains its hold upon the people. The same great actors, Koshiro, Mitsugoro Bando, and Kikugoro continue there, doing their famous roles in the traditional style, and are training their sons to take their places when they themselves have become too old to act. Kabuki is great theatre, and it was a pleasure to see crowded houses every time we went. The auditorium and stage are unusually large, the stage filling one whole end of the theatre. The seats are expensive for Japan (eight yen) and performances last from 3 p.m. to 10 p.m. What goes on behind the Kabuki stage is always thrilling, though little known to the public, which is rigorously excluded. I had been backstage many times before, but I was delighted to see that, the first time they went, Harald Kreutzberg and Friedrich Wilckens (with whom I was giving concerts) were as excited as I was. The gorgeousness of the actors' costumes, the artificiality of their elaborate makeup, the neatness of the Japanese dressing room, the exquisite properties, and the efficiency of the costumers and stage hands could not fail to impress anyone—either in or out of the theatre.

In Osaka we saw the famous doll theatre—a form of Japanese theatrical art older than Kabuki. Many of the plays as well as the dances and movements of the dolls have been incorporated into the Kabuki theatre. The doll theatre is quite different from any Occidental marionette theatre. Each doll is handled by three men, one man manipulating only a given part of the doll. The operators can be seen from the waist up. To a Westerner this technique is at first quite distracting; but one soon becomes so absorbed in the drama, and the men handle the dolls so expertly that one even forgets they are dolls. The stage in this type of theatre is different from the ordinary one. It is oblong with a low ceiling. A narrator and a musician sit on a platform near the audience. The scenery often changes as quickly as in the movies. Zoe Kincaid, who has been giving a series of interesting lectures in Tokyo on the Japanese theatre, has made translations of the doll plays, and she is hoping to bring the doll theatre to America in the near future.

The Noh theatre is also still very much alive in Tokyo. We saw a fine performance at the theatre especially designed to produce only Noh dramas. This performance was not attended by a large crowd, but Noh drama has never been popular. Only the intelligentsia are its faithful devotees. The audience, composed of refined and cultured-looking people, seemed to be more interested in reading the text of the plays than in looking at the actors. The plays are apparently exceedingly difficult to understand even for the Japanese. I became hypnotized with the intense rhythm of the strange voice, the slow, studied walk of the actors, the dramatic expression of the masks, the clean precision of each gesture. There seems to be no fear at present that the Japanese will be allowed to forget the Noh, the Kabuki, and the doll theatre.

We saw the ancient Bugaku dances, which are presented once a year at the Meiji shrine. These dances are given today exactly as they came from China during the Bugaku period. The music is pure Chinese, extraordinarily beautiful and strange, and unlike any other music heard in Japan or China today. Always performed by four men, they are slow, solemn dances, done in costumes with long, heavy trains and great, wide sleeves. This worship of the past, this clinging to old ideals, is at the same time the great strength and the great weakness of the Japanese stage today. So much of the original meaning of certain symbolism and gestures is now completely lost that only the empty form remains. It is indeed very decorative, but often in-comprehensible. The following is a quotation from the English program note describ-ing a very fine dance which we saw in the Kabuki theatre performed by Mitsugoro Bando and his son Minoske:

This play seemed to have meant much when it was written about 100 years ago, but the meaning is now obliterated. Two fishermen appear on the stage and make an attractive dance. In the course of the dancing, the good and evil geniuses come down from the sky, and the fishermen become possessed by them.

It seems quite natural that the youth of Japan, brought up in the very modern cities of Tokyo and Osaka, should desire some new form of theatre and dance which would express their age. Great as is the ancient Japanese theatre it has reached the climax of its perfection. The fantastic demons of Kabuki and the unreal onagatas are now interesting mainly as fascinating museum pieces, which by all means should be kept on exhibit.

Japan now takes her entire modern culture from the West. Except for the daring exaggeration of our skyscraper architecture, Osaka looks very much like Chicago. Without the speed and intensity which make New York and Chicago so dazzling, without the soul which makes our jazz enticing, Tokyo buzzes with American commercialism and with American movies. Tokyo now has a European orchestra of Japanese men looking chic in their tailcoats and playing the best European music extremely well and correctly, but again without inner understanding. The old East is practically gone. Japan stands on the threshold, her feet glued to her rich past, but her ambitions all soaring toward industrial and commercial success. The rare poetry of Japan is disappearing, and she has not yet understood the innate beauty and grandeur of our strident civilization.

The Imperial Theatre was the great hope for a modern Japanese theatre. It preserved the work of the past, but at the same time proceeded logically into the future. Unfortunately the Imperial Theatre was a financial failure with the coming of the industrial depression and now we can only hope that American movies, jazz and revues will not completely destroy the great theatrical artistry of the Japanese people.

America and Europe now take modern dance so much as a matter of course that it seemed strange to arrive in a country which had seen so little that could be called modern dancing. For any European dancer to appear in Japan is a unique experience, however. The Japanese handle publicity in a most expert way. Performers are photographed throughout the day and also during performances. Kreutzberg and I found photographs of ourselves enlarged to life size in the entrance of Tokyo's largest dry goods store. In our honor the top floor of the store was entirely devoted to an exhibition of enormous dance photographs from all over the world. It was great fun after our concerts to have the dance fans backstage and bring us the pictures which they had taken during the performance. They always gave us the pictures and had copies for themselves which they asked us to sign.

Japan is not only photograph mad, it is also autograph mad. After autographing at the theatre until all hours of the night, we were stopped in the streets for more autographs or "sign" as they say. If the Japanese know no other word in English they always seem to know the word "sign."

Before concerts in America one of the most tedious affairs is the light rehearsal, which always takes about two hours. But in Tokyo so efficient are the electricians that such rehearsals are finished in half an hour. Both Kreutzberg and I felt that we had never enjoyed such splendid light effects as we had in Tokyo Kaikan, where we gave our first concerts. We changed our program every night, and in spite of language difficulties, which were tremendous, there were seldom any mistakes made.

When we came back after our tour in the provinces to give three farewell concerts in Tokyo, we noticed a change in the audiences. At the first few performances the audiences infinitely preferred our older and lighter dances. The Japanese are inclined to prefer light, colorful dances with much movement and beautiful costumes. At the end of our engagement, however, they appreciated the more serious dances. Our audiences were composed mostly of the intelligentsia. We were told that modern dance does not as yet appeal to the great masses. The same people came night after night to our concerts, and we felt that there is a real modern dance public growing in Tokyo. The dance and music critics are extremely interested. They seem to remember more of the dancers' careers than the dancers themselves do. They seize upon every little detail and write amazing biographies of the visiting European and American artists.

Unfortunately we did not see any modern Japanese dance recitals, although we visited many schools and saw many photographs of what they are doing. Most of it seemed too greatly influenced by Europe and America. Among the schools we visited was the Eguchi School. Mr. and Mrs. Eguchi had been studying in the Wigman School in Dresden. They and their pupils know most of the Wigman exercises and do them most correctly. However, the Wigman exercises do not seem to lend themselves to the Japanese body. Nor do the toe exercises of the ballet.

It is possible, however, that the study of various European and American forms of the dance will help to free the young Japanese dancers. If they are not taught to imitate slavishly, these studies may help them to evolve modern forms of their own. They are now going through a phase which at first sight seems not too promising, but which may contain the material that will eventually lead to new forms, and which, through international contacts, will really express modern Japan.

The Dance: London Style—An American Ballet Mistress Reports on the State of the Art in England

[In *The New York Times*, June 13, 1937]

Ruth Page, premiere danseuse and ballet mistress of the Chicago Opera Ballet, has recently returned from a series of solo appearances in the Scandinavian countries, said to be the first such venture to be undertaken by an American dancer. While she was abroad she took occasion to see something of the work of her European colleagues, and the following is her bird's-eye view of the scene in London, now said to be the center of interest in the world of the academic ballet.

(Above): The Rake's Progress. (Below): A Wedding Bouquet. Photos by J. W. Debenham.

"Tradition—tradition—tradition!" shrieks London, and the dancer from across the ocean opens the door to what appears to be almost a museum dedicated to the classical dance. England believes that modern dancing came into existence because some dancers were physically incapable of ballet dancing or were too lazy to master it, and concludes that therefore modern dancing is completely amateurish and only for the dilettanti. It is true that technique for modern dancing can be mastered more quickly than for ballet, and one must admit that modern dancing does attract many amateurs. But that the British public condemn the whole field of modern dance for this reason seemed quite unbelievable to me.

After the first shock of this revelation is over and after a few days' acclimatization to this "closed door" atmosphere, one begins to slip back into the past, to the Pavlova era, even to the pre-Pavlova era. The descent is hazardous, provocative, and soul disturbing. But once having hit the bottom, one looks around, no longer so disturbed, as one begins to understand these amazing people, with whom one wishes to live longer.

We go to the Sadler's Wells Ballet and the curtain rises on *Giselle*. At first we smile—it really is very funny—but gradually we smile no more as we are drawn to this quaint old story of the peasant girl who goes mad and dies because her princely lover must marry in his own class. In the second act Giselle rises from her grave and is initiated into the group of "willis," young women who, being betrothed, perish on the eve of their marriage and, according to Slavonic tradition, whirl through their mystic rites unable to find rest in their tombs. Giselle's lover comes to the grave and she embraces him spiritually and lightly for a moment, but at dawn she must return to her grave, and he holds her, stiff and dead, in his arms. This story is certainly sentimental, old-fashioned, and the classic conventions of the ballet are quaintly ridiculous. But the audience is moved by this ballet, and isn't this the true test of theatre? With all our modern sophistication, our upset world of today, how pleasant to return to an old graveyard and watch the "willis" floating around!

This ballet should really be in the repertoire of every opera company, although I would have laughed at this idea if anyone had suggested it to me in America. I had forgotten how theatrically effective some of these old ballets are; that they arouse the same absorbing interest and appeal in the same way to an audience as does the story of the play. However, I must confess to having been very bored with Tchaikovsky's *Nutcracker*, presented "in its entirety," as the program said. It would be an excellent ballet for children at Christmastime, but here at the Sadler's Wells was a grown-up English audience seemingly enjoying every minute of it.

I can't say too much about what splendid work the Sadler's Wells Ballet is doing in London, and my complete admiration goes to Ninette de Valois, the director of this organization. When Miss de Valois left the Diaghileff ballet about eight years ago she felt that the time was ripe to establish in London an all-British ballet, and it is due to her and to the amazing organizing ability of Lilian Baylis that this theatre came into being.

The ballet gives two performances a week. Opera is given on the other days, in which the ballet also dances. I went many times to this theatre, and at practically every performance the house was sold out and the audience always shouted and cheered for everything. I admit I found the audience somewhat indiscriminating, but it must be encouraging to the English dancers to be so greatly appreciated by their own people. The theatre is not situated in the regular London theatrical district, and it has adopted a price scale for tickets of fifteen cents to $1.75 for the best seats; it has developed its own audience of real ballet lovers.

Sadler's Wells has a repertoire of both old and new ballets. Ivanoff and N. Sergeyev have done the old ballets in the old way, as the English do not believe in changing anything from the sacred past, and Miss de Valois and Frederick Ashton create all the modern ballets. In addition Miss de Valois now does most of the teaching in the school connected with the theatre and also dances herself. Her work as choreographer, dancer, and director is marked by freshness, clean-cut style, precision, and charm. Her best ballet, I thought, was *The Rake's Progress*, to music by Gavin Gordon. All the English dancers, including the Sadler's Wells company, apparently worship the Russian ballet and all its traditions. But *The Rake's Progress*, I thought, had a distinctly English flavor which I liked.

Frederick Ashton's ballets at the Sadler's Wells are extremely witty and amusing and often very poetic. His new ballet *Wedding Bouquet*, to Lord Berner's music and Gertrude Stein's words, is a most delectable and refreshing bit of nonsense, quite surréaliste in treatment. All his ballets are based on classical technique but are modern in feeling, and he has a quality distinctly his own. The dancers in the de Valois company show excellent classical training and some have real talent. Margot Fonteyn made a lovely Giselle. Robert Helpmann was always good in parts requiring miming and dramatic style, and Harold Turner is a brilliant and charming ballet technician. Mary Honer has a Lydia Lopokova-ish quality, and Pamela May, June Brae, and Ursula Moreton were always good in minor parts. William Chappell, a dancer in the company, has done some charming scenery and costumes for several of the ballets.

In spite of the reputation of the English as being very cold dancers, the classical ballet is admirably suited to the English temperament and character. I found Alicia Markova a truly great classical dancer of the old school. She is homely but extremely distinguished. She is very cold, yet at the same time her classical dancing has a thrilling quality to it. She is at her best in *Lake of Swans*. Anton Dolin, her partner, is also a fine dancer, but I found most of their large repertoire very uninteresting. Markova does a solo dance called *Water Lily*, in which she moons about in some chiffon, and in this even her exquisite line and poise could not move me.

I saw the Markova-Dolin Ballet in the provinces, both in Nottingham and Edinburgh, and in each city they play every night for a week and give two matinees. They always seem to have good houses and great success, so I conclude that their repertoire is what the English public likes. Nijinska is now the ballet mistress of their company, and it was a pleasure to see a revival of her chic little French ballet, *The House Party* [*Les Biches*] of Diaghileff days. The London *Times* found this ballet "as out-of-date as a ten-year-old milliner's catalogue," but I thought it was by far their most attractive ballet.

One should not go to London without seeing the work of Marie Rambert in her charming little Mercury Theatre. The stage is so small that the dancers do not appear to best advantage, but one simply overlooks the theatre's limitations and becomes absorbed in the fine work which the dancers are dong. Rambert herself gives them a good classical technical foundation, and also gives the young English choreographers a chance to try their wings. [Miss Page's travels were continued in the following article.]

A Dancer Glimpses Europe

[In *The New York Times* "Music News," August 12, 1937]

. . . Her most talented protégé now is Antony Tudor, whose ballet to Gustav Holst's "The Planets" shows a real flair.

One cannot leave London without saying a few words about the extraordinary Cyril Beaumont. Every dancer should visit his charmingly messy and marvelous little shop in Charing Cross Road. Be sure to take lots of money, because you will want to buy everything in the store. Mr. Beaumont not only translates and publishes old books and documents concerning the dance, but writes and publishes books about all the present-day dancers who perform in London. He is now preparing a book which will tell all the stories of all the ballets, old and new, of every country.

I spent only two days in Germany, and in Breslau I saw an all-ballet program, the

Cyril W. Beaumont. From the drawing by Randolphe Schwabe.

pièce de résistance of which was the new Mohaupt ballet, *Die Gaunerstreiche der Courasche*, an exciting and amusing theater piece with excellent music. The company did not have first-class dancers, but at least Breslau has its own ballet. I wish every city in the United States could do as well. However, nearly all the ballet companies in Europe are subsidized by the government and are connected with the opera houses, working all the year round. The dancers do not make much money, but they make enough to live on, and a ballet company is considered as important in Europe as a hospital or school.

An all-ballet program at the Berlin opera was a great surprise to me, because it was exactly the kind the Roxy Theater in New York might give. It was called "Dances Around the World" and the ballet master, Kelling, has trained the girls marvelously. They can do ballet, acrobatic, modern, character, tap, etc. The great success of the evening was the New York scene with tap dancing. The German tap dancers performed in very American style, and the audience went wild.

In Florence, I saw the La Scala all-Respighi program which ended with *The Birds* with the full La Scala ballet, and the choreography adapted from the La Scala choreography by Margherita Wallmann. This was also done in our best Roxy manner, with fountains of real water and an enormous egg which came up out of the floor and out of which hopped the La Scala ballet children all dressed like little chickens.

I saw rehearsals of the Sartorio Ballet in Florence, but unfortunately could not stay for the performance. Czobel and Bergeest, formerly of the Jooss ballet, are the excellent soloists of this company. Sartorio is to be commended for keeping this company together, as Italy is an extremely difficult country for the dance.

In Paris I was surprised to see the ballet *Cinderella*, which I had commissioned from the French composer Marcel Delannoy for the children's performances at Ravinia Opera in 1931. It was given at the Opéra Comique and was charmingly but conventionally choreographed by ballet master Tcherkas. We saw the thirty-seventh performance of this work!

In my own solo recitals in Norway, Sweden, Denmark, and Finland, which were, I believe, the first appearances of an American dancer in the Scandinavian countries, I was surprised to find large audiences responsive to the most modern dances in my repertoire. *Tropic* and *Possessed*, for example, which contain simple though somewhat unusual stylized primitive movements to Indian and Brazilian music, were invariably applauded more enthusiastically than the more conventional dances. In these northern countries, though they have seen very few of the large ballet companies, the solo dancer need never be afraid of his most serious work being over the heads of the crowd.

Not every country accepts the solo dancer. For example, the taste in England seems to be entirely for large ballet groups. Even Kreutzberg, who is so completely adored every place in the world, was not a success in London three years ago.

In Norway and Sweden there is a serious and interested dance public open to new ideas and evidently not clinging to tradition. But Copenhagen is still extremely classical. Germany, in so far as I could gather, likes every kind of dancing. The Russian ballet is a tremendous success there and at the same time Kreutzberg and Wigman and Palucca are more popular than ever. The modern dance has not yet dawned in Italy, and Paris is still faithful to the Russians and to Serge Lifar at the Opéra. I saw no ballets any place with social content. The people in Europe, and even in Russia, like their dancing as an escape from everyday life. The more glamorous and theatrical their ballets, the better they like them. Perhaps in America, where life is not yet too hard, we do not feel so strongly the desire for escape, and therefore seek a dance form derived more directly from the experiences of our complex and chaotic world.

The Dance: Among Latins—A Few Notes on a South American Tour . . .

[In *The New York Times*, July 28, 1940]

Ruth Page and Bentley Stone and a contingent of twelve dancers from the Page-Stone Ballet have recently returned from a Latin-American tour with an opera company. Besides appearing in the regular opera ballets, they also present complete ballet programs. In view of the recent interest in South and Central America as a field for touring dance companies, Miss Page's notes are of particular interest.

Our Latin-American neighbors love ballet dancing. They remember Pavlova, and it is hard to convince them that there is any style of dancing other than Pavlova's. Pavlova's repertoire consisted mainly of the usual standard classical ballets, each performance invariably ending with a set of eight or nine divertissements which included one solo for Pavlova, a duet for her and her partner, and group numbers by the corps de ballet. My first experience in dancing outside this country was with the Pavlova company on its last tour of over a year in South and Central America.

But times, if not the public's taste, have changed since Pavlova's day. Any ballet company going to South America now has the competition of inexpensive movies, which the people can see for seventy-five cents, while a ballet company must charge a large price even to make expenses. For example, the Opera and Ballet Company with which we have just played for one month in Caracas, Venezuela, charged $11.00 for each orchestra seat. A ballet company must be absolutely first class to win popular favor at such prices.

Caracas is probably the most expensive city in the world because the country is on the gold standard and, as almost everything is imported, one has to pay fabulous

Ruth Page and Bentley Stone in Caracas, Venezuela, 1940.

prices for just ordinary necessities. About the only thing we discovered which is not expensive is dancing lessons! There are three local foreign teachers, who are only able to charge about $1.00 for class lessons. But their classes were flourishing, and there seems to me to be a great field for dance teachers all over South America. Miss Stahl was brought by the Venezuelan government from Vienna and teaches gymnastic dancing in the schools Mr. Dimitri is an American and Miss Galli is the inevitable Russian dancer without a home.

They all say that the South American dancers are very lazy and very "dilettante-ish," but that they have a great interest in dancing. Stage people all over South America are still *déclassé*, and "nice girls" just don't go on the stage. They get married very young and have children, and a career for a woman is almost unheard of.

Still the people adore dancing and are an eager audience. They do not hesitate to show their feelings and are quick to both shout and hiss. Their taste definitely runs to "toe" dancing and by far our most popular ballets were Schubert's *Love Song* (which is sentimental and poetic) and Dance of the Hours from *La Gioconda* (which is nothing but a technical display).

My dance *Tropic* interested the critics and the "avant-garde" (which is small) in Havana, Curaçao and Caracas, where, surprisingly, it caused quite a stir. But my dance *Delirious Delusion*, a comic surrealist dance which is successful in even the smallest towns in the United States, was hissed. It is, of course, always dangerous to do comic dances in any foreign country, as each nationality laughs at different things; and Latin-American taste definitely runs to the pretty classical ballet.

An amusing feature of an artist's experience in South America is the very florid wording of the typical review in the daily newspapers. This quotation is from *El Heraldo* of Caracas:

It is useless and very difficult to praise the actuation of Ruth Page's Ballet. Those dancers are wonderfully inspirated and in the voluptuous rhythm of the dance they give us the sensation of a beautiful dream. Something as if we enjoyed the charm of a dream where the opium would make sculptures of temptress grace and visions of sublime creatures of another world. Each presentation is a new success for the Page-Stone Ballet.

I am very happy to have had a chance to introduce our ballets in the beautiful Teatro Municipal of Caracas. To me it is one of the loveliest theatres in the world, and the fact that the fleas like it too, and that the plumbing is very primitive, actually did not bother much. The Venezuelan government, unlike ours, takes a great interest in and spends a lot of money on art, and this country should have a marvelous future. And their welcome to the foreigner whom they like is unforgettable.

Havana boasts a progressive club called the "Pro Arte Musical." I gave two concerts there under its auspices eight years ago and returned there this spring with my partner, Bentley Stone. Besides bringing artists from abroad, the organization runs a dancing school in the Pro Arte Building, and every year it gives ballet performances with all the pupils in the beautiful Pro Arte Theatre. The ballet master is a Russian named Georges Melanoff and the school has about 175 pupils. The pupils pay $2.00 per month to become members of the association, and for $1.00 additional per month they are entitled to four lessons in the ballet school.

The Ballet Caravan, the Jooss Ballet, and Kreutzberg have all recently danced in Havana, but it seemed to me after talking to many people that the Cuban taste has not changed or advanced since I was there eight years ago. In fact, it seemed to me on this, my third, visit to Latin America that in this respect nothing has changed much since Pavlova's day.

I think all of South America now needs a lot of good dancing teachers, and it is a tremendous field for pioneer work. Many of the leading dance organizations are going there these days, and all the public needs is an opportunity to learn what has been going on in the dance world for the last twenty years.

Most of South America is in about the same state that the United States was in twenty-five years ago. Its peoples look almost entirely to Europe for their culture, and they have not yet sought much at home for material for their art. Now, if they should

fight as hard for their artistic and cultural freedom from Europe as they did in the past
for their political and physical freedom, a new and extraordinary culture should come
there that would be a complement to our North American civilization.

Europe has been cleverer than we have been in handling our South American
neighbors. Partly because of this they look much more to Europe for their culture
than to us. But now that Latin-American relations have become so extremely
important, there is sure to be a *rapprochement* and a continual interchange of art and
artists between North and South America.

Blessed by the U.S.O.—Tale of a Happy Union Between a Company of the Page-Stone Dancers and the Sailors of Our Armed Forces—Across the Footlights

[In *The Dance*, May 1942]

It is a long trek to the big concert room at the end of the navy pier, and according to
Chief Miller it is easier to keep track of the whole navy than it is to hold together our
group of lovely young ballerinas who had come to give a performance for the sailors.
Not that our dancers do not have a perfect discipline too, when they don't their tutus
and get up on their points. But the sudden meeting of sailors, ballerinas, spring, and
full moon over the lake seemed to be too much for both sides.

To be admitted to the Chicago Navy Pier is like being suddenly catapulted into
another world—a world to me like Mars might be. They gave us buttons to wear but
they didn't open any of our luggage. I would have thought that if they go to the
movies at all, they should have suspected some of us dancers of being spies. But no
questions were asked and we went on.

The pier extends a mile and a half out into the lake and you look back on our city's
tall grim buildings with an air of superiority because you feel you are now at last a part
of the war effort. You are admitted to the world of men marching, the hustle and
bustle of building and of exciting and mysterious things going on which most of us
girls do not understand very well.

It did not seem too auspicious to me, after we finally arrived at our destination,
when we were told to be very careful of the stage because just last week an acrobat
had fallen through a loose board. Also, when I looked at the tinny old upright piano,
which some kind soul had graciously donated, I did not feel that our classical music,

Bentley Stone in *Punch Drunk.* Photo by Dorien Basabé.

even played by our brilliant Ruth Gordon, could make much of an impression. The stage had no backdrop and no front curtain and all of us girls dressed together in a freezing room with dim lights. Also, the performance had to be given in broad daylight, or rather broad twilight, and for all those who do not already suspect it, let me tell you that we dancers are not half so glamorous without floods, spots, and lots of softly shaded gelatins. But one thing that really thrilled my soul (and it is not an overstatement) was to have sailors for stagehands.

Well anyway, there we were, all dressed up for 2,000 sailors and we took bravely off, nobly escorted by Mozart, Ravel, Liszt, Schubert, Smetana, and our own Chicago composer Laura Aborn. Bentley Stone made his first appearance in *Punch Drunk.* The boys understood immediately, laughed heartily, applauded vociferously. After that Mr. Stone dared appear in tights (my maid always said that just to see Mr. Stone in tights was worth the price of admission to any theatre) and all during our poetic *Du Bist die Ruh* of Schubert, the boys were completely quiet and attentive. I revived for the occasion one of my very first creations, *The Tight Rope Dancer*, a saucy little number in which I am very giddy. In this dance I have as my assistant a little Frenchy maid, by name Marian Moss, and I felt that probably the delighted screams of the sailors were aimed as much at her as at the hardworking little circus performer (me). We ended up with another revival, Ravel's *Bolero*. The WPA kindly lent us a drummer for the occasion and this helped us to weave our spell.

The sailors are of course all young, and they like the dancers to smile and be gay. A lot of sailors have never seen a ballet before, so you naturally cannot expect an audience of great subtlety. But what they lack in subtlety they make up in interest, curiosity, warmth, and friendliness. They are happy that you have come to dance for them, and so in the end everyone is happy.

After the performance we ate. Dancers love to eat, and we thought the navy food was fine. Liverwurst, salami, American cheese, wholewheat bread, pie, cake, coffee.

Then Lieutenant McMillan asked if we wouldn't do a little "stunt" for them in the officer's bar. Two of our fifteen-year-old girls, Marilyn Haight and Jackie Drije, volunteered, and with their little stomachs quite full (I'm sure) they did such a succession of acrobatic stunts that I, who had always thought we were a company of extremely serious classical dancers, was more than amazed. They flew through the air with flipflops and butterflies and stood on each other's shoulders and were utterly beguiling—and all improvised and unrehearsed. Our second pianist, Madeline Dahlman, played infectious music with such a light spirit that she was asked to stay and play some more after the dancers were winded. It all ended by one of the officers obliging with a song, and on the dock we watched a Brooklyn gob jitterbugging. Then we went home in army station wagons.

These boys are doing so much for us. They are learning a lot too, but some of them (particularly those southerners who find the Navy Pier extremely cold) are homesick, and I hope that there is more that all of us can do for them.

Paris, 1950—
The American Invasion: Revenge [1950]

Paris is seductive in the spring, with its smiling friendly countenance, its flowers so ravishingly combined by florists of real imagination, its *fraises de bois chantilly* (wild strawberries covered with the thickest, softest, yummiest whipped cream in the world), its wines, its inexpensive perfumes, its apparent leisure to live; but like all seducers, the serpent lurks beneath! In this case the snake turned out to be a group of French dancers who were apparently determined to take their revenge on the first American ballet company that came to Paris, in retaliation for the treatment they received in New York in the fall of 1948.

Serge Lifar headed the Paris Opera Ballet that came to New York. The demonstration, with American dancers picketing, was held *outside* the theatre on the street and was against Lifar, not as an artist, but because he was accused of collaboration during the German occupation. At that time the opera stagehands refused to work if Lifar performed, so Lifar was suspended for a couple of years. But Paris apparently forgives and forgets easily, and Lifar is back in his old position as god of the opera ballet, dancers, choreographers, practically everything. The Paris Opera Ballet is France's pride, and when it was received adversely by the New York press, the French were furious. Many people in Paris told me about a man named "Jean Martain" who they said "despises French dance art." In fact, John Martin told José Limón jokingly just before our departure that there would be a retaliation in the Paris press for his bad reviews of the French dancers.

So we, the innocents, happily arrive, having been invited by the Bureau de Concerts de Paris, to show the French public some *American* ballets. They wanted only one program, but Katherine Dunham advised me to take a second program as "the French public is completely unpredictable in its taste." Katherine also warned me (as did Helen Dzhermolinska of *The Dance Magazine*) that it is customary to give a party for the critics before the opening. "However," she said, "if you don't and if you get bad reviews, at least everyone will say you are an honest woman." We did not give a party. However, a week after we opened the critics who had

Les Ballets Americains arrives in Paris, 1950.

Ruth Page and Bentley Stone pose about Paris in *Frankie and Johnny* costumes. Photos by Lido.

written well of our performances asked to call on me. I found them extremely interesting, well-informed, and delightful to talk to. I made a terrible gaffe by saying that Paris had really not seen much that was new in dance, and this remark was resented. Why, Paris has seen *everything*—*everything* comes to Paris!

Choice of Program

As always, the program is difficult to choose for a foreign country. The ballets were decided upon, and then the company was chosen to fit these particular ballets. In other words, the ballets were as carefully cast as a Broadway show and as carefully rehearsed. It was really a unique company, many of our corps de ballet having been stars in other companies. Of course, having stars in the corps de ballet does not necessarily mean a good corps de ballet, but I prefer interesting individuals in companies to Rockettes any day. Like a Broadway show, we should have had a week on the road, but this was impossible due to the expenses, and so our corps was better at the end of the run than at the beginning.

The company was definitely affected by the hissing on the opening night, but it made me want to hiss right back. José Limón's *La Malinche* and *The Moor's Pavane* are certainly first-class examples of modern American dance, and *Frankie and Johnny* is real folklore Americana. I knew that Limón would be perfect as King of the Ghouls in *The Bells* and that Pauline Koner would be a seductive Bathsheba in *Billy Sunday*.

One could perhaps criticize our program for lacking unity of style, but there can be an interesting unity in diversity, and for the kind of ballets that I have always done I need ballet dancers who can do modern dance and modern dancers who can do ballet. In the only ideal dance company that I ever directed, the Chicago WPA Dance Project in 1938, we had a modern group, a ballet group, and those that could do both. Betty Jones, for instance, as well as dancing the lovely Desdemona of Limón's *Moor's Pavane*, sang in the pit in *La Malinche*, sang and acted one of the three drab Salvation Army sisters in *Frankie and Johnny*, and danced on her toes as a Golden Bell in *The Bells*. Lucas Hoving, starring in the Limón ballets, was versatile enough to be able to step into about any part in *Frankie and Johnny* in case of illness. And Pauline Limón sang nightly in *Frankie and Johnny*. So the Limón group was not a separate entity by any means.

The most modern of interior decorators do not consider it necessary anymore to adhere always to one particular style. For instance, an ancient Chinese painting fits perfectly into a modern room, or good examples of period furniture can be effectively used against the simplicity of a modern background. A few years ago, this would have been heresy. In any event, as I think back on our Parisian programs, Limón's *Moor's Pavane* seemed to me to represent classic art, while *Frankie and*

64

Johnny kept reminding me of the poetic realism of Faulkner. This ballet seems to be sordid in a very poetic, sort of comic way. How differently one judges one's work in a foreign country!

By the time we got to *Billy Sunday*, the French audience took it right in their stride and didn't bat an eyelash. Also, by that time we had the good sense to have a French actor explain *Billy* and *Frankie*, and this was a big help. The management insisted on having both *Billy* and *Frankie* on the same program from then on. Our management made some mistakes with us certainly, but on the whole they were extraordinary. Dussurget and Lambert are not at all commercial managers like most of the managers in our country, but they want always to give their audience something new and interesting.

We took *The Bells* (with new Remisoff costumes and retaining the Noguchi set) in deference to Darius Milhaud, the great French composer. *The Bells* was supposed to open the program, but Milhaud refused to conduct the opening ballet, so our management put it at the end. Obviously, Limón could not open the program, nor could *Frankie and Johnny*, so we were forced to open with *Scrapbook*, which had to be changed. *Scrapbook* was supposed to begin with *Variations on Euclid*, a six-minute ballet which was so successful at our tryouts that the management insisted on putting it at the end (as the French public always comes late, they would not see it!). A solo that I choreographed for Talley Beatty to Villa Lobos's music was not permitted on opening night, nor was my solo *Tropic*, nor any of the Page-Stone comedies. On our later programs, these excluded dances were all *real* hits (with the exception of *Tropic*, which I could never get up the nerve to do). So the *Scrapbook* on the opening night was entirely different than it was planned. As anticipated, *Variations on Euclid* was a great success and continued in the *Scrapbook* every night, as did an eleven-minute version of *Americans in Paris*, closing the *Scrapbook*.

The *Scrapbook* (along with *Frankie and Johnny*, given every night) was not such a *potpourri* as one might imagine, as it was a specially designed ballet with a scrapbookish transparent front curtain which closed between dances and opened on to an abstract background suitable for any kind of dance. At the end this abstract background rises, revealing another painted backdrop for our ballet *Americans in Paris*.

This ballet featured three black dancers, Talley Beatty, Alex Young, and Albert Popwell. I had really combed New York to find interesting black artists and these three boys were the result. They danced in all our ballets (except Limón's); they were the three devils in the new version of *Billy Sunday*, while Billy was danced and acted by Bentley Stone (and Kenneth MacKenzie in two performances). Alex Young was the bartender in *Frankie and Johnny* and also danced in the corps de ballet in *The Bells*—in which Dorothy Hill and Kenneth MacKenzie made a handsome and dramatically convincing couple. Bentley Stone and I danced *Frankie and Johnny* every night of the three-week run, although it was erroneously stated in *Dance News* [July 1950, pp. 10-11] that *Frankie and Johnny* was taken out after the first performance.

One could be shocked and irritated by the booing of the French dancers, but the real shock to me was the completely inaccurate reports that got into the American press, most of which we did not read until our return. Helen Dzhermolinska in *The Dance Magazine* was the only one who reported the story accurately. Tom Fisher and I were both accused of saying that Lifar "had organized the cabal against us." This is completely false, as even if we had known it to be true we certainly would not have said so to the press. In the various letters and conversations that ensued, we were told that the Paris Opera Ballet had organized the booing squad and that was all. *Time* magazine gave the most inaccurate account of all and really seriously damaged our reputation here. It even misquoted *Le Monde* as stating that *Frankie and Johnny* was in the worst of German taste. One would think that even a news reporter would know that *Frankie and Johnny* could never, no matter what you think of the ballet, be considered German. *Time* also said that the booing continued the second night. To be accurate, there were two boxes filled with hissing, but these few people were scarcely heard at all due to the cheering of practically the entire house. Also, *Time* only reported Merlin of *Le Monde*, who got in by subterfuge on the opening night, and not *Le Figaro*, a newspaper just as important, whose critic came to the second performance, the night on which all the critics were invited.

In Paris, there is a strange custom that the management invites all the elite of Paris to sit downstairs, while the balcony is sold, and no critics are admitted. The dancers of the Paris Opera Ballet got Merlin in, and he made a scoop, his notice appearing the next day, which is almost unheard of in Paris. His notice was devastating, and as usual a lot of people believe whatever they read in the newspapers and it was difficult for us to get a fair chance after such a beginning. The leading radio critic quoted *Le Monde* on the radio, giving us a bad review. But after he had seen our performance he completely changed, saying "it was an excellent performance" that everyone should see.

But there are things in Paris that are just as difficult for us as the booing French dancers and the opening night audience of elite vipers. Rehearsals in Paris, it seems, are an open invitation to any photographers and newspaper reporters and critics who choose to wander in. For some unaccountable reason our pictures, carefully taken in America, cannot be used and *each* newspaper or magazine must take its own. If we could have gotten into our costumes and makeup and had the lights and sets and had them all taken at one time and finish with it, that would have been fine. But no, each paper wanted different poses, different costumes, and different ideas.

Never could we rehearse alone! Fortunately, our repertoire was well rehearsed before we left New York, but there are always replacements in a ballet company at the last minute. We all suffered terribly from the cold in the theatre. One boy, Jean Nettles, went to the hospital for about the entire season with pneumonia (we left him in Paris, however, as the premier danseur of the Folies Bergères). The weather was lovely outside the theatre, but inside was always like a cold, dark church. The press always seemed to see us at our worst—tired, dirty, working under bad conditions. In the rehearsal room downstairs was such a terrible piano that Simon Sadoff, our pianist, had to sing all our music, or we couldn't recognize even the simplest of it, and all our scores are very complicated modern ones. There was another studio at the top of the Champs-Elysées Theatre Building, where the piano was not too bad, but the floor was fixed for making recordings in that room, so that it was all squashy and soft. On toes, one felt as though one were hiking over the hill, and I don't like to hike in toe shoes!

Incidentally, the French as a whole hate modern music. They apparently are only beginning now to appreciate Brahms. However, the men in our orchestra prepared our extremely difficult modern scores with great care, under the direction of Emerson Kailey, a highly gifted young American conductor, who has spent the last five years in Paris introducing American music to the French public (mainly over the radio). Simon Sadoff conducted Limón's two ballets and sang with just the right feeling the Villa-Lobos dance for Talley Beatty. We really had only one complaint in our musical setup, and this we knew about in advance. There is a quaint French custom that if a member of the orchestra does not wish to come (for any reason) to the rehearsal or performance, he sends a substitute. We tried to arrange for this in our contract, but a French custom is a French custom, and no rules in the world can change it. On Saturday nights half our orchestra were substitutes. On those occasions we shut our ears, counted, and prayed!

Bentley Stone and José Limón do not speak French. José became adept at saying, "Je suis charmé," and said it on all occasions. Bentley gave the company class, did his performances, and said nothing. This left me holding the bag, so to speak, and I had to answer all questions, make all explanations, hold all the interviews, talk over the radio, and handle all public relations matters. This I had certainly not counted on, and my French is quite feeble but was better than anyone else's. It wasn't so difficult to explain my own work, but when it came to *La Malinche*, I wanted to be really very explicit about Limón's ballet. I started out explaining carefully the predicament of the downtrodden Mexican peon and Cortez's conquest of Mexico through the help of "La Malinche," and I waxed eloquent on José's treatment in dance terms of this interesting situation. In spite of all my efforts, no one listened attentively until I said, " 'La Malinche' was Cortez's mistress." After that, my explanation of Limón's interpretation of Cortez's conquest boiled down to that one simple line!

Now I understand why Roland Petit has *ten* public relations men—I never really knew what the words meant before, as I have never even had *one* publicity man. One of Petit's tribe of ten came to me to ask my opinion of Petit's *Carmen*, which I didn't mind giving because I happen to like most of it very much. If I hadn't liked it I would have said so too, as I am accustomed to making enemies. It seems that few of the Paris critics liked *Carmen* or *Oeuf à la Coque* when they first opened in Paris, but in spite of the critics these ballets seem to be here to stay, and the Marigny Theatre seems the ideal setting for them. Petit has added *Les Demoiselles de la Nuit* to the program, which greatly strengthens it. After questioning me, his public relations representative was going on to ask Lifar his opinion of *Carmen*. Great excitement in Paris, because it seems Petit is to be asked to do a ballet for the Paris Opera.

French Gôut

Our next problem was the famous French taste. We had tryouts at the dress rehearsal in the studio and let the management pick our first program. They had invested so much money in us, and they knew the French public so well, that we felt we should take their advice. Unfortunately, they did not pick some of our later hits. The Rambert Ballet running at the same time at the Sarah Bernhardt Theatre did the same thing. It was their first appearance in Paris, and their *Lady Into Fox*, which in every other country was their *pièce de résistance* (according to Marie Rambert), was a complete failure in Paris. We did not see it till the second night, and two-thirds of it had apparently been cut out. The night I was there, it seemed to me that their two most successful ballets were Tudor's *Judgment of Paris* (which they did delightfully) and *Gala Performance*. These are of course familiar to us. Of their other choreographers, Walter Gore seemed to me to be outstanding.

A howl went up when we four girls for *Americans in Paris* donned our costumes, which were designed by Remisoff as caricatures of four crazy American girls with foolish exaggerated costumes and hats. We all thought they were amusing and original, and our sharp Gershwinesque movements suited the extreme cut of the costumes. The French read deeper meanings into what we had done as a light satire on the giddiness and homesickness of the Americans in Paris. Even the title now sounds a little ominous to the French. Well, it seems that our French friends considered these costumes an insult to the *haute couture* of Paris. (Actually they were an insult to the American female!) American women, it seems, usually wear French clothes in Paris, and these costumes, they thought, were a cruel satire on French clothes. So the management had Georges Wakhévitch design and hastily execute four tutus with big hats, which were very cute, but all four of us looked so completely French that I just *couldn't* do the American style steps in mine. So we wore the old ones until I had time to train my understudy for my part. Then, Limón's costume for the King of the Ghouls was considered too grotesque, too ugly for such a handsome man as José, and they thought the Othello costume in *The Moor's Pavane* was not rich enough—that it needed jewels on it. The only thing we changed was the headdress for the Ghoul King, which Wakhévitch designed very interestingly, keeping it ghoulish in spirit.

The French, as we all know, do have perfectly wonderful designers for both scenery and costumes. I don't believe any artist had appeared yet in Paris as great as Berard, but in practically all the theatres one does see beautiful and magnificent scenery. In America most of us couldn't possibly afford such complicated sets. In *Les Demoiselles de la Nuit* (about half an hour in length), there are three elaborate sets and a front curtain, and as New York knows, Petit's *Carmen* also had many complicated and expensive sets. Our taste, even without regard to money, is much simpler. Practically every newspaper in New York spoke of Noguchi's beautiful skeleton of a church, which he made for *The Bells*, and Noguchi's stunning sets for Martha Graham are greatly appreciated in New York. But not one Paris newspaper mentioned Noguchi, who is, I think, our greatest designer for the dance.

None of the newspapers mentioned any of our music either—in fact they talked about practically nothing but *Frankie and Johnny*. It hit them very hard indeed. The same people came many times to see it and either loved it passionately or hated it in the same manner. Bentley Stone's and my version of *Frankie* is much closer to the original Chicago production than the Ballet Russe de Monte Carlo version, which has become somewhat more balletic. The following list of the things that shocked Paris was in one of the French newspapers with pictures to illustrate, and this list was really a great surprise to all of us. Here it is:

1. The daring manner of this dance (*Le côte hardi*)
2. Frankie's red hair
3. Johnny's purple shirt
4. Dance with the coffin (a coffin is apparently tabu on the French stage)
5. The placing of the corpse in the bier (*la mise en bière*)
6. Nelly's lily wreath
7. Macabre parody
8. Frankie making effects with her legs over the coffin
9. Salvation Army girls drinking beer over the bier
10. All the dancers dressed in "earth colors"

So now, at least, we know what caused all the sensation!

And after all these troubles, why did everyone love Paris, and why do we all want to return? Mostly, I liked it for the wonderful and intelligent letters I received about our performances and for the people who came backstage to see us—artists, writers, students, even a lot of French dancers, among them Le Corbusier, Goncharova, Larionoff, Escudero (who was fiery in our behalf), Jean Jacques Etchevery, ballet master of the Opéra Comique (who seemed most sympathetic to our efforts, and whose Friday all-ballet nights we unfortunately were never able to attend), and Alexander Volinine, who is very proud (and I don't blame him) that his figure is exactly as it used to be in his dancing days as Pavlova's great partner. Volinine has a fine school but, due to our frantic schedule, our company was able to go to him for only one lesson. Volinine was very disappointed that Limón did not come to the lesson. I tried to explain that modern dancers have a different way of practicing. "No matter," answered Volinine, "classic dance basis for *all* dance." We were something very new and different for them and they seemed more than delighted to welcome us. I was glad they liked Limón and his company. It seems that neither Wigman nor Kreutzberg ever had any success in Paris, so introducing modern dance was somewhat risky.

To me, Limón seems practically a classic in the modern movement, and I could think of no two better ballets than *La Malinche* and *The Moor's Pavane* to lure the French public to an understanding of our American modern dance. There are some in Europe who persist in thinking modern American dance is Germanic, and one French paper thought Limón's art was distinctly Japanese. But anyway, they accepted it, and I think giving one ballet of his at a time instead of a whole program was highly advisable. A couple of times we tried giving two Limón ballets on the same program, and the management said it was too much. It is wonderful that Paris will see Martha Graham in June, and the fact that the Baroness [Bethsabee de] Rothschild is sponsoring her, that she only has five performances and thirteen ballets, and the fact that Paris is waking up to recognizing America as an important contributor to dance art, should guarantee her the success she so vastly deserves.

"Les Ballets Américains" gave twenty performances, while the Rambert Ballet gave only ten in a theatre half the size, and even the Sadler's Wells gave only ten. Incidentally, the French didn't like a lot of *their* costumes either. I don't really think the French opera dancers will ever boo in an organized effort again—at least not at modern dance. Their devotion to Lifar is really touching. I asked one of the corps de ballet girls (when they were in Chicago) how they liked Balanchine at the Paris Opéra, and she answered, "*Il est bon, mais Lifar* (and her eyes lighted up), *il est pour nous!*"

Another reason we loved Paris was because of our amazing managers, Dussurget and Lambert. They made it tough for us at first when they were educating us in French taste, but two more attractive and interesting managers certainly could not exist. It was they who brought Menotti's *The Medium* to Paris. It was beautifully done, but was apparently a failure with the public. However, they are now negotiating to bring *The Consul* to Paris. In the summer they have organized one of the most interesting music festivals in Europe at Aix-en-Provence, their program for this summer being most imaginative.

70

We certainly started in Paris with a nasty hullabaloo, but we ended on high C. The only thing wrong with our Paris season was the extremely inaccurate and vicious reporting of the American press, sacrificing everything for a sensational story. But how can one not love a country that recognized Poe and Faulkner before we did? Fortunately, we knew nothing about the false reports until our return to New York, and *that* was a big shock indeed!

It is not the vipers in this Parisian paradise (and almost everyone admits it is the world's most alluring city) that one needs to fear—it is the insidious and seductive French influence that seems to affect all artists who stay there. We all know about the "French" painters such as Picasso, Modigliani, and Chirico, "French" writers such as Rilke and Hemingway, and the "French" dance group *par excellence*, the Diaghileff Ballets Russes!

Diaghileff's desire to "*épater*" the Parisians led to some exciting experiments, but ended in artistic sterility. One wonders what would have happened to Balanchine had he stayed there. Certainly in Paris he would not have created the healthy new ballet style that he has invented for the New York City Ballet Company. Balieff, like Diaghileff, fell, to his detriment, under the French influence after a two-year run in Paris with his Chauve Souris, and the lovely Katherine Dunham returns to New York in an extremely attractive show, but now more French than black.

With all the minor misunderstandings, dance seems still a much simpler international language than the spoken word. But the audience, with the help of the *unbiased* writers, must probe beneath the surface and try to get at the core of the artist's work. And what a wealth of new material can result from the impact of one nation's art upon another if the artist bewares the pitfalls and is not afraid of new inspirational sources. What a perspective one gets of one's own country while living the strangeness of new environs and suffering new emotions!

Seagulls and Swans, London, 1952

The walk from my hotel (the Savoy) across the bridge to Festival Hall was a source of constant enchantment for me. Nothing in London was quite as I expected it to be. First of all I loved the climate. The temperature was mild (the English thought it cold), and it did not rain at all. But what I liked was the mystical light that hovers over and around London. The Thames, as I crossed it three and four times a day, never looked the same—the swans were floating on the flowing water and the seagulls were swirling around, and inside the hall where we were rehearsing I was trying my best to get the dancers to feel the swoops and swirls of my *Merry Widow* ballet (called *Vilia* for the Festival Ballet production).

The English dancers were also different from what I expected. I thought, of all things, they would be perfectly disciplined. Actually they are no better disciplined than the Champs-Elysées Company, and most of you know what I think of French discipline! Also, contrary to expectations the English dancers are not at all cold—in fact they are full of temperament and dance with great verve and abandon. In fact, they do one ballet, *Symphony for Fun*, exactly as though they were Americans dancing in a Broadway show (and this is a compliment). Another wonderful thing about Festival Hall (this contrary to expectations also) is the food. Imagine! You can have tea and coffee at all hours of the day and night and simple but excellent dinners at reasonable prices both before and after the performance. To me it was such fun to be able to eat and drink in a theatre that I was forever snacking and I came away from London much fatter than when I arrived from Paris.

I had heard so much about Christmas pantomimes, and now was my chance. *Jack and Jill* and *Dick Whittington* seemed to be the most popular ones. I sat through both of them and except for the slight fairytale-ish story that ran through both of them, they are greatly like old-fashioned, fast-moving, big-production-number vaudeville, and I was very disappointed. However, at the Players Club I saw *Babes in Arms*, a real Victorian pantomime and I thought it was delicious—the same sugary story, the leading boy character played by a girl, the leading comic played by a man dressed as a woman (this seems to be the rule), but such funny puns and such an amusing

Oleg Briansky in *Vilia*, London Festival Ballet production, 1952.

combination of acting, singing, and dancing (choreographed by M. Charnley—a very talented young man). Dolin was appearing as star of *Where the Rainbow Ends*. He really did look young and handsome, and the audience loved him.

Wherever you go in London (at least in the holidays) it is impossible to get away from the good and bad fairies. The good fairy always wins in the end, and I really thought that maybe I too might meet a good fairy in my daily walks over the dreamy Waterloo Bridge. And what do you think, I finally did meet one, just like in the fairy tales. I was going to the farewell performance of Festival Ballet for which every seat was taken. They ended with a very dashing and sparkling performance of *Prince Igor* (Vasili Trunoff is a real successor to Bolm and Woizikowski) with a huge chorus singing.

After the performance I went backstage. Just outside the royal box, which had been occupied by Princess Marie Louise, there was Marie Louise herself looking for all the world like a good fairy in white ermine and pearls, giving a lovely speech of farewell to the company, bidding them good luck on their journey to Paris. The dancers were still in their *Prince Igor* costumes and looking like a hoard of real savages juxtaposed to the Princess and her pearly ladies-in-waiting. I really couldn't believe my eyes and ears at first. It even seemed to me that the Princess had a wand and was touching us all with her enchantment. And then it all disappeared in a fluff of London fog, and now I am on the ferry bound for Paris.

We Who Travel—The Director of a Widely Touring Midwestern Ballet Company Talks of Theatres, Food, Buses, and People

[In *Dance Magazine*, June 1967]

A ballet tour is an exciting adventure with people and places, packed with problems. Every day is a challenge. My newly named International Ballet travels by bus, and we dance in six different cities every week. I have traveled all over the world in all kinds of transportation (even by donkey), and one of the nicest ways to travel is by bus. The bus takes you directly to your hotel and to your theatre and becomes a sort of traveling home.

You have to pick your seatmate very carefully, you have to pick your reading material so as not to have too much or too little, and you have to bring books that are thought-provoking. Then you have to learn to "quirl" up comfortably and relax and sleep. Most of my sleeping on tour is done on the bus, and we have a lot of fun as well as a lot of time to sit and think, "What is this life so full of care that there is no time to sit and stare?" Well, you have it on the bus. The bus also gives me a chance to get acquainted with my company, and I find their various personalities fascinating to study.

Two rather mousy little dancers surprised me one day by finding a book sale and returning with so many books (on Southern architecture, metaphysics, and all kinds of unusual subjects) that the rest of us could hardly get on the bus. One of our ballerinas traveled with a bird who enjoyed perching on people's heads. We finally had to eliminate from the bus all but human animals.

Ruth Page's Chicago Opera Ballet on tour, 1960. Melissa Hayden, center, and Ruth Page on right.

Besides learning to feel at ease on the bus, one has to learn to pack abstemiously. I eliminate and eliminate, as I find carrying my own luggage very tough. On this tour I took one white fur coat, which I admit looked very sad at the end of the tour, three dresses, one pair of trousers with coat, and too many books.

The dancers are naturally concerned with floors, drafts, and keeping physically in shape. Two hours before each performance we have a slow warm-up class which lasts an hour and a quarter. This is a ritual I enjoy more than the dancers do, as I sit all day on the bus and watch the performance from the front every night. The performances are particularly stimulating to me when there are cast changes and when I find a dancer who unexpectedly gives something new to a role. Also it is interesting in the new ballets to see how the dancers develop roles from performance to performance. My dancers try just as hard in the small towns as in the big cities, and sometimes the audiences are more discriminating in the smaller places.

I enjoy meeting the local dancing teachers and the local managers. The latter are unusual people who work very hard to develop an audience, and who try to bring artists of quality. They are succeeding.

The level of teaching in this country has improved tremendously since my day as a dancer, and now ballet is taught along with modern dance in a number of universities. This is important, as dancers today often have to be equally proficient in ballet and modern. When I was a director of the WPA in Chicago in 1938 I had a group of ballet dancers and a group of modern dancers, and I managed to use them successfully in the same ballets. But my choreography has always been in very free style, employing any movement that to me seems to express what I am trying to say. The free mixture of ballet and modern of the young choreographers of today pleases me, as it is what I have always tried to do.

A big problem on tour for the dancers is what and when to eat. The food in the United States gets worse and worse everywhere. I asked a leading French actor who had just returned from a tour of one-night stands what he thought of American food. He said, "I thought it was wonderful." I was very surprised and said, "What on earth did you eat?" "Cheeseburgers, three times a day," was his reply. And that is about it. If you stick to cheeseburgers, you don't do too badly. But even they are usually inferior. Dancers eat a big lunch and then they don't eat again until around midnight. Usually only night clubs are open at that hour, and to find a place to stay open for us is quite a problem. Sometimes parties after the performance are nice, but we have finally become brazen about accepting. We now say, "We'd love to come if you will feed us."

Our most important problem, however, is the physical aspects of the theatre. Sometimes I think I would like to line up all the architects who have designed theatres in this country and shoot them. In practically every theatre there are serious mistakes. The greatest mistake, of course, is trying to build a theatre that will serve as a gymnasium at the same time. When the floor in the auditorium is perfectly flat, nobody can see the stage. When there is the proper rake and the theatre is not too big, one's enjoyment of a ballet performance is increased 100 percent. We spend a fortune on toe shoes for the dancers, and I rarely get to see their feet. During the eleven years that we have toured (for three months every year), there is hardly a city or a town that we have missed, and I am happy to say that every place we have appeared we have been asked to return many times. But some of the theatres are appalling, and it's always the architects' fault.

There are certain theatres that stand out as particularly awful, but certain ones that we remember with affection. I will not list the awful ones. Almost the best one we have ever danced in is the new Jones Hall in Houston. Here our performances really looked wonderful, and I cannot begin to say what a difference a proper stage and lighting means to my ballets. I suppose this is true of any ballet company, but it seems especially true of mine, and I suffer agonies when we perform in an inadequate theatre. However, when the audience loves us even in a bad theatre, then the pain is less. The new theatre in Seattle is a wonderful place to perform, and I also liked the new Frank Lloyd Wright Theatre in Tempe, Arizona.

One gets many surprises on these tours. In Moorehead, Minnesota, there is a perfect small theatre for dance. It is called the Center for the Arts, and I can imagine spending the rest of my life working in this enchanting little place. The theatres in San Antonio and New Orleans are much too big and have an arena atomosphere. The audiences in both places are extremely receptive and enthusiastic. But the audience can't see from most of the seats, and I am surprised that anyone will go to these theatres for a ballet performance.

Another theatre of which I am especially fond and where we have danced many times is the Municipal Civic Auditorium in McAllen, Texas. Have you ever heard of McAllen, Texas? This is a place that really pleases me. Grand Prairie, Texas, has a bright, shining, comfortable, new high school auditorium, which should attract all the touring dance groups. Topeka, Kansas, has a marvelous audience, but the theatre there is so dreary. The Music Hall in Kansas City is extremely comfortable and has splendid modern equipment. I will never understand why the architects cannot make a theatre with charm and taste and comfort. I liked the theatre in Carbondale, Illinois. The backstage is crowded, but the auditorium is sympathetic and is properly raked, so that the audience can see. It is one of the few places where we had a small audience, but they made up in enthusiasm what they lacked in size. This was our first performance in Carbondale, and I would like to return.

Clowes Auditorium in Indianapolis is also one of the best theatres in the country. Out of sixty cities, the ones I have mentioned are the only ones on this tour which were inspiring. Frank Hale's Royal Poinciana Playhouse in Palm Beach is an attractive theatre, but the seating capacity is uneconomic for us, and it is so busy that it's almost never available.

I thought the theatre in West Palm Beach where we have performed about six times was impossible. But the last time we were there, Les Grands Ballets Canadiens were also in town and I went to see them. The audience was full of titled English people and rich Americans, but the auditorium where I saw them was even worse than the one in which we performed. There was no place for the orchestra, so they used a tape, the floor was so slippery that two girls who fell were taken to the hospital, and the stage was so small that in *Les Sylphides* the dancers could hardly move at all, let alone dance.

The question of repertoire is of utmost importance on these tours. If I had any sense I would take one program only, but this is too limiting for me so we keep changing programs. Columbia Artists in New York, our booking agent, always wants me to make the programs out with proper casting in the middle of the preceding summer, and as we do something new every year, we never know whether the new ballets will be successful. Over the last twelve years our "Operas-Into-Ballets" have been extremely popular, but having danced them so many times over this long period I am now starting to drop them from the repertoire. It is so difficult to find music for ballet, and so many of the operas furnish ideal music. What better composer could one find for ballet than Verdi or Rossini or Richard and Johann

Strauss, for example? The problem of transforming operas into ballets is a tremendous one, involving insight and imagination, and musical purists often object when we dance to music written for singing. I find the dancing body can successfully replace the singing voice. But today it seems silly to even think of this when one considers that practically anything from a Beethoven quartet to any old beep or burp goes for ballet music. Anyway, my "Operas-Into-Ballets" have been put to rest for a while. I only hope we will have as much success with our new repertoire.

When I say that I find touring in this country extremely provocative, I don't mean to say that I would rather go on these tours than stay in one place in a nice theatre with a nice studio in a nice community and "create" like a great many of our companies are able to do these days. But for want of something better I am happy to have the chance to tour.

I think in the last dozen years our company has done more to popularize ballet in the United States than any other company, and this is a satisfaction to me. Our company has been able to exist because from September to the middle of December we have always been engaged by the Chicago Lyric Opera. A lot of dancers do not like to dance in opera, but I have always found this work alluring, especially now when all the modern directors use ballet in almost all the operas. Again, I don't say that I would not rather spend my time doing important big ballets, but I have managed over the years to find a great deal to interest me and my dancers in the opera. Unfortunately, the opera does not have enough money or interest to give all-ballet programs, although we have given a few very successfully. In my opinion opera and ballet should go hand in hand (as in the Gluck and Monteverdi operas), but the opera people do not think this way.

So I do what I can with the problems we have here in Chicago. The Lyric Opera season has been canceled this year due to financial problems with the orchestra, and McCormick Place, where for two seasons we have danced in a big production of the entire *Nutcracker*, has been burned down and we are in serious trouble. We are hoping to find another theatre for our annual *Nutcracker* production, but as this particular production was designed especially for the enormous stage at McCormick Place and with an audience capacity of 5200, it is difficult to find any place else where we can use this production. A twelve-week tour in 1968 has already been booked for us by Columbia Artists, and now my problem is to see what we can do this fall. Does anybody need a ballet company?

Gone with the Wind—Avignon Festival, Summer 1968

The mistral seems to blow harder in Avignon than anyplace else, and I ought to know, as I live in St. Tropez in the summer and Chicago in the winter. In St. Tropez there are endless discussions among the natives about what happens when the east wind blows, when the Sirocco comes hot from Africa, when the north wind in one night scatters all the seaweed and the pebbles out to sea and leaves a clean sand beach. These variable winds affect all the life in southern France. The other day I sat in the Cour des Papes in Avignon, watching Tania Grantzeva give a splendid two-hour class to Béjart's dancers. Sometimes I thought the wind would literally sweep the dancers away, and at night during the performance it blew through the wild hair of the male dancers (the girls wore their hair neatly tied up), shifting emphasis from Béjart's choreography and giving it added dimensions. The mistral blows one's thoughts around too, and these are my thoughts on my two stormy nights in Avignon in August.

The dancers of Le Ballet du XXe Siècle are exhausted after a month's season in Avignon, and Béjart, while watching Grantzeva's class, said there were so many outsiders in the class that he could hardly find any of his own company. Rosella Hightower's daughter, an exquisite little girl (aged thirteen) and Elvira Braunschweig (a long-legged fourteen-year-old) were struggling valiantly with difficult steps. Mme. Braunschweig will send her daughter to Russia for four years to study. She was considering New York, as her daughter is a Balanchine type of dancer. She would certainly get good classes, but there would be no one to take care of her, whereas in Russia every five or six girls have a guardian who looks after their education and well-being (and probably their politics too!). Massine's son Lorca was in class also. He has a rather disorganized technique, his body being somewhat gangly and out of proportion, his face small and ascetic and framed by long black hair. He is, however, a fascinating personality and one that I will never forget. While he seems to be a lazy dancer technically, I would say that he is full of choreographic ideas. When he was about eighteen years old I saw a whole program

Maurice Béjart at Avignon, 1967.

of his creations at the Recamier Theatre in Paris. It surprised me. Instead of modern youth ideas, some of the dances were of the scarf-waving Isadora Duncan type. What will be the influence of Béjart on him?

Béjart is quite a law unto himself. In about 1952 I saw his *Symphonie pour un Homme Seul* in Paris. I thought to myself this is certainly an interesting young man, but Paris offered him no opportunities. Like Marcel Marceau (whom I had seen in a tiny theatre on the top of the Théâtre des Champs-Elysées with about ten people in the audience), who had to succeed in Germany and England before Paris would even look at him, and like Margot Fonteyn, who divides her career into B.A. and A.A. (Before America and After America), Béjart found an artistic haven elsewhere, in Brussels at the Théâtre de la Monnaie, which at the time was dying of malnutrition. He gave them such a shot in the arm that now he can have anything he wants from them. I saw his performance of *Romeo and Juliet* in Lisbon early this June, after which Béjart asked a moment's silence for Robert Kennedy, "victim of dictators and communists."

Some of the audience started singing the *Internationale* (Portugal has been under the dictatorship of Salazar for forty years) and Béjart was immediately arrested and dumped at the border and his company had to leave Portugal at twenty-four hours' notice. The Lisbon performances and the Portuguese tour were canceled and the Gulbenkian Foundation, which was sponsoring Béjart's performances for the spring music festival and was reportedly planning to start a ballet school in Brussels, immediately withdrew its support. The Théâtre de la Monnaie had to take the entire loss for the canceled performances.

In Avignon, Vilar (who has run the Avignon Festival for twenty-two years) and Béjart, both considered very left wing, were condemned by the enragés, who shouted "Down with Vilar, Béjart, and Salazar!" Which side is Béjart on? Like Barrault, he seems to play on both sides.

Vilar brought the American Living Theatre for the festival in Avignon, and they made so much trouble that the mayor finally, with great difficulty, banished them. I understand the story as follows:

Le Chêne Noir is an unimportant local dramatic company that was performing near Avignon in a play called *Paillaise aux Seins Nus (An Old Bag With Bare Breasts)*. This was forbidden by the censor, and then all the trouble started. Le Chêne Noir had nothing to do with the festival. Le Living said they would not perform if Le Chêne Noir could not perform and they wanted Vilar and Béjart to cancel out the whole festival in sympathy. The latter two very sensibly would not do this. In *La Messe [Pour le Temps Present]*, a full-evening ballet which requires quiet and concentration, the actors walked on stage and demanded that Béjart explain why he didn't stop the performance immediately. It was difficult to tell the enragés and actors from the dancers, as they were all wearing blue jeans. Finally, the police carried the demonstrators away and the performance continued.

Le Living gave *Paradise Now*, which disgusted the citizens of Avignon so much that the Mayor asked them to change the program. They responded by performing the censored play in the streets and howling and yelling till 3:00 and 4:00 a.m., keeping everyone awake. Le Living want complete freedom of expression for everyone to do anything they want. Some of them lived in one room at the chic Hôtel d'Europe and the management there reported that they were so dirty that the room had to be completely redecorated. The management heaved a sigh of relief when they left, and then they came back! A number of French newspapers accused Le Living of creating all the commotion just to get publicity for their forthcoming American tour. Well, they got what they wanted, especially when they all lay down in the streets in front of the theatre trying to prevent the audience from entering. Of course, I am dying to see them, aren't you?

This was all quite sensational after the *dolce far niente* of St. Tropez, where all the excitement consists of Bardot playing boules in the Place des Lices, Dolin arriving with his handsome Yugoslave protégé, Igor Koask, and Roland Petit in the port with his fourteen-year-old daughter. She is studying ballet at the Paris Opéra, but she says, "I will write and paint too, in case my dancing career is not a success." Her father has always represented real Parisian chichi. He chooses to have his ballets designed by the artist of the moment—always le dernier cri with Roland. The choice of the directorship of the Paris Opéra seems to be between Petit, who represents tout Paris, and Béjart, who represents the people. If I were Béjart, I would stay in Brussels, where he can produce anything he wants, rather than go to the Paris Opéra, which will probably always be honeycombed with intrigue (even though they have marvelous young dancers).

The night I left Avignon, Le Ballet du XXe Siècle had intended to give a performance on a small island in the Rhone for 20,000 people, free of charge. I did want to see again their best male dancer, Paolo Bortoluzzi, Germinal Cassado, a fascinating actor-dancer, and Jorge Donn, an unforgettably expressive creature. One notices the girls in that company much less than the boys, but Laura Proença is a dancer of exquisite delicacy and Marie-Claire Carrié, Tania Bari, Duska Sifnios, and Hitomi Asakawa are all worth notice. Maina Gielgud's talents have been well-exploited also, but it is the Béjart boys that one remembers. Well, I did want to see them all again, but the mistral blew their stage away, and nothing was left of it except a little piece of wood sticking up in the middle of the Rhone. Better the stage than the dancers, I suppose!

Fairyland [1971]

What would we girls do without our gay friends? They do not fall in love with us, but they *love* us—they really do. They like to go out with well-dressed women, and they take a great interest in what we wear. They love to dress up themselves, and most great dress designers are homosexual. How beautiful they make the women look. I have noticed one thing peculiar to all of them. No matter where you go with them, they tend to bring you home and ditch you completely after midnight. Then they go off on their own—to gay bars, I suppose—and they never ask you to go with them. A woman can never be a part of their mysterious rituals, and heaven help any female who falls in love with one of the boys—they cannot be changed. They are for friends, for fun, and mostly for artistic life. When you spend most of your time with gay boys and then go out into society with straight men, how exciting it is! How sexy you suddenly feel!

Gays fit perfectly into the world of ballet and are a godsend to ballerinas (especially to ones who have husbands or lovers). Imagine doing a pas de deux with a sexy

heterosexual who desired you. There is such close physical contact, so many intimate intertwinings of the male and female bodies, that sexual involvement can easily become predominant. But with a homosexual partner there can be a physical indifference that allows both dancers to concentrate on the art of the dance and forget about sex. Quite a nice situation, I would say, as a pas de deux is serious business and requires sometimes a lifetime to be perfected.

At rehearsals it is amusing to watch dancers working. They like to look in the mirror all the time, and of course the ABC of partnering is for the man to look ardently at his lady most of the time. Gay boys feign this ardor and they cannot be looking in the mirror or at the audience. Alonso and Youskevitch (completely heterosexual) were the ideal man and woman relationship, and their pas de deux were completely satisfying. However, it is often difficult to tell which partners are not straight, so skillful are homosexuals at dissembling. That is the magic of the theatre.

In any event, there are not more gay boys in the dance world than there are in the literary world, or even in the business world. Long ago I went to a concert of Artur Rubinstein in Monte Carlo. Diaghileff was there, and when he got up to leave a whole line of his obviously flitty boys followed him out. At first I thought, "How disgusting," and then I started to laugh. Sex is for fun, and today homosexuality is fashionable, and everything is out in the open. Well, the boys have suffered long enough, and we should be grateful to them, as they do not increase the population. Vive les boys!

Ballet Festival in Venice

[June 14 to July 6, 1975]

I have just spent three weeks in Venice, during which time there have been fifty-six performances of eighteen ballet companies. This, plus all the beauties of Venice, is almost too much. Two weeks before this festival opened, the people who live in Italy thought the festival would never take place. I hand it to the Italians that in most respects it has come off brilliantly.

The performances have taken place in four locations. The Piazza San Marco is certainly one of the glories of the world, but I was always glad when performances

Piazza San Marco, Venice.

there were rained out because you cannot see the stage from any one of the 4,000 seats. I went there to see Béjart's *Ninth Symphony* (which is appropriate for a large open space) and Petit's *Notre Dame de Paris* (which is a big spectacle). These are popular works and I would have liked to really see them.

The Teatro Verde on the Island of San Giorgio is a perfect out-of-doors theatre. You can almost lie back in the seats, there is a rail where you can put your feet (this is heaven for dancers), and sight lines are excellent. Such a lovely walk through Italian gardens to get there, but if you are rained out (which is what happened to the Ballet de l'Opéra de Lyon) heaven help you. The boat service in Venice is of course efficient beyond belief, but in a wild crisis like this, everyone panicked. The Ballet de Lyon had just started a work called *Venise Secrete* (by their director Biagi) based on Venetian music from the fifteenth to the eighteenth centuries. The title intrigued me enormously, and I wanted so much to see it. The critics condemned it after seeing only two short movements, which I felt was unfair.

The Ballet Rambert from London had better luck and gave an excellent perform-ance in the Teatro Verde. I had not seen Rambert's company since its changeover to modern dance, and I was impressed with the artistic approach. American choreographers have been very influential in this company. I especially liked Falco's *Tutti-Frutti*.

The third out-of-door theatre is in the Campo del Ghetto Novo. It is a very interesting neighborhood, and the people watching the stage from their apartments are most picturesque, but the audience can't see much unless they are in the front row. Béjart's new mudra school (located in Brussels) gave a performance there. The school sounds fascinating when you read about it. There is no tuition, and people are chosen for their talent.

This school is supposed to teach practically everything about the theatre (multimedia, of course) and the performance included a bit of everything, even eating spaghetti, but the main theme was "Acqua Alta." This happening was created for Venice (although the program listed Béjart as choreographer), where water is certainly queen. "Venice, risen from the water, enriched by the water, slowly devoured by the water."

I saved the best theatre till the last—La Fenice. It was partially burned down, but the inside was redone in 1850 in eighteenth century style, and is completely charming in every detail. I saw there *A Cedrus* given by the Budapest Opera Ballet—a full evening by the company's choreographer, Laslo Seregi, and this is a real period piece with enormous decor and elaborate costumes. It was full of symbolism. Guessing what it was all about was fun, but I really didn't know till I got home and read the program, which was certainly full of surprises. The cost of bringing such a big ballet to Venice would have been prohibitive to any of us poor Americans. These government-subsidized theatres (and all of them are) really support the dance in a big way.

I was so happy that Milwaukee-born and Chicago-trained (Stone-Camryn) John Neumeier is having such a great opportunity as director of the Hamburg State Opera Ballet. If he had stayed in Chicago or even New York, his talent could never have been developed. I saw his *Romeo and Juliet* (six or seven years ago) when he was still director of the Frankfort Ballet, and made arrangements for him to choreograph it for our Chicago Lyric Opera Ballet. I thought his financial arrangements extremely reasonable, but finally it did not work out. I have learned from long experience that Chicago is the most difficult city in the world to get things going in. Chicagoans are timid and don't trust their own taste, and they must be sure that what they are getting has been approved everyplace else before they can accept it.

Well, Neumeier is now really approved by most and I find his work poetic and intriguing (quite Germanic in feeling). His company (many Americans in it, among them Truman Finney of Chicago, who is his first star) were supposed to dance Mahler's *Third Symphony* in Piazza San Marco, but they were rained out, so it was transferred at the last moment to La Fenice at 10:15 p.m., where La Scala Ballet of Milan had just finished at 9:30 p.m. The latter was somewhat disappointing, although

Pistoni, their choreographer has a few clever ideas. Later, I saw the "Hamburgers" in a program at the Ghetto Novo. *Dammern* is a very sensitive interpretation of Scriabin's music. One of Neumeier's best ballets is *Die Stelle*—a dreamlike evocation of Crumb's music. *Sacre du Printemps* ended sensationally with a solo of the Virgin entirely nude, powerfully danced by Beatrice Cordua. I wonder what Chicago would think of that.

Easily the maddest juxtaposition of people on the same program were the Iranian gymnasts Zour Khane and the Original Hoofers from the United States. The latter have been seen on American television and it was refreshing to see such honest frankly entertaining old boys doing their stuff. I was glad to have seen the Iranians, for they were asked to leave Venice for political reasons and did not give their second performance. I found these huge powerful men doing fast coupé turns, and wrestling to a kind of chanted poetry very unusual, and I have never seen anything like it.

I missed the Ensemble National du Senegal, but these black dancers certainly looked beautiful in their exotic street clothes wandering around the streets of Venice, and they fitted perfectly into the landscape. I also missed Antonio Gades Spanish Ballet in Lorca's *Bodas de Sangre*, but I did of course see this great dancer when he danced with us at the Lyric Opera. I did *not* miss Wayang Wong of Bali in stories of the Ramayana, and they took me back to my beloved island of Bali where I spent so much pleasurable time studying with their greatest dancer and teacher, Mario. Les Ballets Jazz (Montreal) added nothing new to this form of music.

I was delighted to get a chance to see the Tokyo Ballet, because I had heard so much about the precision of their corps de ballet, and in that I was not disappointed. But when the curtain opened on Balanchine's *Palais de Cristal* it took me a long time to get used to the short legs, the big heads and the smiling faces of their very un-Balanchinian style. Ronald Hynd's *Orient-Occident* with music by Xenakis didn't really come off, but it seemed a step in the right direction, and was full of interesting movement. Felix Blaska's ballet *Concerto* of Prokofiev showed the dancers to best advantage. Blaska had the courage to have all the dancers doing the same steps at the same time (very unusual these days) and here the Japanese precision really showed up. This company was started thirteen years ago by Russian teachers, and if they can find their own choreographic way, this could be a great company. The dancers all looked very happy.

The grand finale of the festival was supposed to be the foursome of Fracci, Kirkland, Baryshnikov, and Bartoluzzi. These days you can't start a performance by turning on the lights or just opening the curtain. You apparently have to see the dancers practicing or fooling around before the set performance starts, so these four wonderful dancers did a sort of barre, and a bit from *L'Après Midi d'un Faune, Coppélia, Spectre de la Rose,* and a few class combinations for no reason at all that

I could see. Then a *long* wait followed by four pas de deux from *La Sylphide*, the inevitable *Don Quixote, Coppélia*, and *Giselle*.

The latter should have been the end, but no—some dancers in the audience came on the stage and started to do barre (in their street clothes) with the four stars. I don't know what this is supposed to prove (the democracy of the stars?) but it was far fetched, and I would have preferred to go home with the memory of Fracci and Baryshnikov in the last segment from *Giselle*. When the famous four bowed to the public, the church bells were pealing, the extras (who had come on the stage to apparently jazz up the finale) were clapping behind the four dancers, who continued to bow to the public accompanied by Albinoni music. Black clouds threatened all night, but no rain. Quite an evening, and I will remember it.

Martha Graham's performance at the Teatre Verde had a very small and uninterested audience, and the garden trellises were not the proper background for her ballets. The Fenice was fine and at the end she had an ovation, which made me very happy. She looked beautiful as she bowed in her flowing green robes, and I was proud to have such a great artist representing America.

I had tickets for the Netherlands Ballet and for the New York Theatre Ballet, but both were rained out. Anyway, I saw enough, as I was beginning to get stale. How do the critics keep their freshness, or do they?

Besides the performances, there was a big exhibition at the Fenice of Serge Lido's exciting dance photographs, and at the Palazzo Grassi a "Homage to the Designers of Diaghilev" arranged by Richard Buckle (from the Theatre Museum of London, not yet opened). Old costumes, usually so dreary to look at, were tastefully draped on statues, and while this exhibition was conceived and executed in six weeks, I found it touching and full of exquisite memories of a great period of dance. Picasso's enormous curtain for *Le Train Bleu* dominated the Palace.

There were dance films every morning at 10:00 and every evening at 6:00 as well as concerts of Balinese and Tibetan music. One could write a book about the school organized by Porcile and under the artistic direction of Hightower and Béjart. Special floors were made for the dancers, lots of showers were installed (I am ashamed to say we don't have any in our Chicago School), and the spacious gardens were a delight. Hightower, Chauviré, Baronova, Grantzeva, Béjart, and Talley Beatty were some of the splendid teachers. I saw no talented pupils in the classes that I watched, but the impetus was there. I am not sure that a three-week course with the pupils changing all the time is condusive to serious progress, but the place is certainly perfect for a summer school.

The festival was sponsored by UNESCO and subsidized by the city of Venice. Probably such an exceptional event cannot soon be repeated—maybe never. I am certainly glad I went.

PART III.

The Art of Dancing

The Dancer as Student—Proving that a Dancer Should Have a Thorough Understanding of Music, Sculpture, Painting, and Literature, if She Would Do Anything of Real Artistic Value

[In *Beauty*, April 1924]

One rarely associates the dancer with the student. This is not surprising, considering that not only the public, but dancers themselves are generally ignorant of the art of the dance. Dancing in its highest form is a combination of all the arts, and a dancer should have thorough understanding of music, sculpture, painting, and literature to do anything of real artistic value.

The amount of research necessary to create a dance is quite appalling, and often the material is limited and difficult to find. Each nation and each period has a style of its own, and to do something that has real form and meaning one must spend hours at the museum and library. Even then, after a tremendous amount of study, for the dancer who has no imagination and no originality it is impossible to create something beautiful or interesting.

It is essential for a dancer to acquire a good classical ballet technique at an early age, as this is the best foundation, both mental and physical, for all styles of dancing. If one has been able to master this difficult and intricate technique, other forms of the dance can be learned quickly. To keep in training a dancer must continue this strenuous practice every day.

Toe dancing is the most fantastic, the most abstract, form of plastic art. It has no nationality and carries us to a realm of pure fancy. The whole idea is to leave the earth, to stand on the very tips of the toes with arms outstretched to the infinite, seeking something away from human passions and human pettiness. The poetic nocturnes, the dreamy waltzes, and the gayer mazurkas of the immortal Chopin have been the inspiration of all toe dancers. However, toe dancing is not limited to this one style—chic minuets, dainty pizzicatos, and coquettish little polkas are delightful when danced on the toes. Then too, toe dancing may be grotesque or humorous—its varieties are infinite, as it is the creation of man's fancy.

Many are the crimes that have been committed in the name of toe dancing. It is a life study to feel as much at ease on one's toes as when walking. If a dancer must think about her feet, her arms become cramped and unbeautiful, and dancing is nothing if the arms are lifeless. The arms must move in perfect coordination and

(Left): Ruth Page in Havana, 1919. *(Below):* "Sweet Peas on tip toe for a flight . . .," Indianapolis, 1917. *(Right):* In *Butterfly,* Indianapolis, 1917.

Ruth Page and
Eleanor Shaler,
1915

harmony with the rest of the body, as dancing must be like a series of beautiful sculptures, each one a perfect pose.

Greek dancing is much easier physically than toe dancing, but to attain that beauty of line and thought expressed so nobly in the sculpture of Greece is not easy. Their expression is human and deep, and often their steps are heavy and seem bound to the ground, while again they leap into the air and seem to take a keen delight in the purely physical pleasure of the free, beautiful movements of the athlete. A wealth of material may be found in the Greek grotesque dances, which seem little known to the American public. The only way to get the spirit of the ancient Greeks is to study their sculpture and drama.

All national dances are called character dances, and we find in a nation's dances the true spirit of her people. What could be more expressive of a race than the gaiety of an Italian tarantella, the humor and strength of a Russian gopak, or the noble and beautiful rhythm of a Polish mazurka?

Of all character dances, perhaps the most interesting are the Spanish dances. They combine a certain austerity of a proud race with the warmth and fire of a people born in a land of sunshine and laughter. For a foreigner to learn to play the castanets and to understand the subtle rhythms of their many dances is a difficult but fascinating subject.

The dances of our own American Indians are full of color and fantasy, while Negro jazz is one of the most interesting of dance rhythms—these are danced principally by men, as the Indian and Negro women dance little. There are few dancers versatile enough to be able to dance both character and classical dances.

Of all the different styles of dancing I think perhaps the Oriental has been the most abused. Anything that is sensuous and colorful is immediately termed Oriental. The East offers a tremendous field to the dancer, but even after a long serious study of Oriental art, at best all we can do is to give a kind of impression of their spirit. Each movement of the fingers, each turn of the head and every twist of the eye has a meaning in the Orient. Their dances mean nothing more to us than a series of beautiful postures, but to an Oriental public a whole story is unfolded. Then, too, their music is so strange to our ears, and their instruments are so different from ours, that it is almost impossible for us to reproduce their music successfully.

Some of the most exotic and interesting dances in the world are performed in Java, Bali, and Siam. For centuries these dancers have carried out the traditions of their ancestors, and from year to year these beautiful dances are performed for the king and his subjects, who sit for hours watching the dancers mime the stories that they know and love so well. Their costumes are rich with gold and jewels—in Siam it takes a dancer a whole day to dress for the evening's performance, whereas in this country the idea seems to be that an Oriental dancer wears as little as possible.

America is developing fast artistically, and if appreciation of dance can grow as rapidly in the next twenty years as appreciation of music has grown in the past twenty years, I think we can count on a large public really interested in this beautiful form of art. The dancer herself has tremendous difficulties to face in the way of education, but now with such great artists and teachers as Michel Fokine and Adolph Bolm the problem has been practically solved.

Dance and Drama

[Speech given in The New York Public Library Music Division's lecture series, "The Dance and Its Allied Arts," on February 15, 1947]

In considering the subject of dance and drama it is well to remember that it was only in Western Europe and only in comparatively recent times that the so-called theatre arts of music and song, of pantomime and acting, and of dancing were split up and used separately for entertainment and theatrical purposes.

From the early ceremonials which led to the birth of drama, the Greek plays, the banquet-balls (which used poetry, declamation, pantomime, and dance), to the commedia dell'arte in Italy, all these theatre arts were fused into a unified performance. So also in the Far East, including both China and Japan, for thousands of years. Right up to the present time, no separation of the theatre arts has ever occurred. No performer there even today is ever considered great unless he is at the same time a great actor, a great singer, and a great dancer—all three!

But about 200 years ago in Western Europe the theatre arts somehow became separated. Orchestras and instrumentalists played music, singers sang, dancers danced, and actors spoke and acted. While there have been partial unifications since, such as the gradual development of modern opera, even in such cases one of the theatre arts has tended to predominate over the others. It is only in the past decade or two that a modern movement has started to re-unite these separate arts of theatrical purposes. Many people tend to think of this process as though it were daring and original innovation, forgetting that throughout most of the history of mankind and over most of the globe, it would never have occurred to any performer or entertainer that dancing, singing, and acting were theatrically separable.

96

Frederic Franklin, Ruth Page and Alexandra Danilova in *The Bells,* Jacob's Pillow, 1946.

So strong have been the forces of separation of the arts that in the popular Broadway theatre of today, it is still considered strange for a dancer to speak or sing. Modern dance has in a few instances availed itself of a narrator or a singing accompaniment, but for a dancer in one of the large ballet companies to speak even a few lines is unheard of. Even in present-day opera, the dancing is usually interpolated and has little to do with the dramatic action or plot of the opera as a whole.

For myself, I have long been interested in a synthesis of the spoken word or song with dancing, and in the use of dancing to enhance the dramatic effect of the theatrical performance of which it forms a part. For the past five years I have been giving solo performances, principally at the colleges and universities scattered across the country, in which I dance and recite poetry at the same time. In our ballet *Frankie and Johnny*, Bentley Stone and I made use of popular song and introduced three Salvation Army girls to sing the words as an accompaniment to the dancing through which the story is told; and in one of my very first ballets, *La Guiablesse*, I used a singer.

At the present time I am working on a still more experimental form in my new ballet *Billy Sunday* . . .

First let me say that it has always seemed strange to me that most American audiences would apparently rather hear an artist talk about his work than see or hear the artist perform his work. Last year, at the Composers Concerts Series at the University of Chicago, I was surprised to find more people at some of the lectures by the modern composers than at the performances of their music the following night. Americans, unlike Europeans, incline to approach art from the head rather than the heart. Sometimes I wonder whether anything can really be said about dancing half so effective as the dancing itself. Modern dancers, they say, talk too much; ballet dancers, too little. As Virgil Thompson, the New York *Herald Tribune* music critic, once remarked: "Ballet dancers are autoerotic and have no conversation."

Certainly I am not alone in this interest in the subject of words with dancing. The Theatre Guild a couple of years ago offered a competition for the best so-called one-act dance-play, in which the dancers would not only dance, but speak. This, as I have said, is quite another matter than the often used narrator, who does *not* dance, but speaks the words which describe the dancing or pantomime. I had several conferences with Lawrence Langner, who runs the Theatre Guild, about one of these plays which he himself had written. Many dance-plays were sent in, and although so far the Guild has not produced any of them, I understand that Mr. Langner's interest remains as strong as ever.

Why is it that, to most people, even a few spoken words in a ballet seem to be revolutionary? To me they seem natural. I sat next to a soldier at a performance not long ago. He had never seen a ballet before, and he kept saying to me, "It is lovely, but why don't they ever talk?" I feel much the same. But you would be amazed what a terrific antipathy there is—not only from both audiences and critics but from the dancers themselves—to this combination of words and dance. I met Massine not long ago, and he asked me what I was doing. I said that I had been giving concerts in which I spoke and danced poems at the same time. Massine, who is the exception in regard to experiments, said, "Oh, that sounds fascinating. You know," he added, "I was in Spain and there was a man who was singing and dancing at the same time, and it was perfectly wonderful." I said, "Oh, I would like to see that. How did it turn out?" He replied, "Well, a month later the man went crazy." As I am only speaking, not singing yet, maybe I am just a little crazy.

Of course, people say right away, "How can you speak and dance at the same time?" I reply that if you breathe correctly for dancing, you can also speak . . .

At this point, perhaps, I should say something about the process of ballet creation and my own viewpoint toward the role of the choreographer. As of course we all know, ballet may be important for its movement, or its music, or its drama. Each choreographer tends to place a different emphasis upon each of these basic aspects; and the difference between choreographers largely depends upon the particular emphasis which each choreographer places upon them.

Many of the so-called modern choreographers primarily emphasize the movement, letting the music and drama take a less dominant place. In other words, frequently the movement itself will dictate the dramatic and other elements in the dance. Possibly it is this lack of emphasis upon the drama or story which makes modern dance seem incomprehensible to some of our audiences. I am reminded of a story my Texas manager told me, about a little girl and her mother who were apparently attending their first modern dance recital in Dallas last autumn. The little girl turned to her mother and said, quite audibly, "Mother, is she crazy?" To which her mother replied: "Shh! I don't know." Many of the so-called classical choreographers, on the other hand, tend to emphasize the music, using the vocabulary of classical movement without strong emphasis on the drama or story.

My own approach might be said to be half-way between the moderns on the one hand and the classicists on the other, in the sense that neither the movement nor the music is subordinated.

If I were to judge my own work, which is always difficult for any artist, I would say that I try to emphasize the drama, or dramatic *purpose*, of the movement. In other words, in my ballets it is the dramatic element which comes first, and in a sense conditions or governs the choice of music and the style of movement, as well as the particular steps employed by the dancers.

Nowadays, dance has become an integral part of musical comedies such as *Oklahoma! Carousel,* and *Allegro*. It was an innovation to use a dance sequence in a Broadway musical to heighten and advance the drama, or at least as an essential part of the drama, with movement alone. This use of dance for dramatic purposes was borrowed by Broadway from the dramatic ballets which preceded it; and in turn it enhanced the demand for dramatic ballets by audiences attending the performances of ballet companies generally. So you will see, I hope, from what takes place on the stage next month at City Center [in *Billy Sunday*], that my purpose has been to create dance movement which will enhance the dramatic effect of the ballet as a whole, as well as the various scenes or parts that make it up. Before I finally complete any role, I cannot feel it until I have worked it out on myself. For this reason, I dance all the roles of all my ballets and create them on myself before training my dancers. This takes time, but it is indispensable to me.

This brings me to a fact which never fails to astonish me—that even experienced musicians and theatre people frequently think that a ballet is created almost overnight, once the idea and the music have been chosen. A member of the Chicago Opera orchestra came to me the other day with two new ballets by an Italian composer named Picciolo. These ballets had been given at La Scala in Italy; and my friend, being an Italian, was anxious to have them put on by the Chicago Opera Company. I looked over the piano scores and librettos, thought them promising, and told him so. As our opera director in Chicago is an Italian, I thought he might be interested in producing them.

My friend then brought me pictures of the scenery and costumes and said, "I suppose you could get one of the ballets ready in three or four days." I let out a gasp and said maybe if I rushed I might be able to get one of them ready in three or four *months*. My friend, being a musician, seemed to think that creating the choreography was as simple a process as reading over the music. The musicians really do prepare a new work in two or at the most three rehearsals. Maybe someday we dancers will have a notation system whereby we can do the same, although I doubt it.

The only real way to record accurately the steps of a ballet is to make a motion picture of it. I will never forget the first rehearsal I ever attended in the Diaghilev Ballet Russe when it was reviving an old ballet in the Casino at Monte Carlo. Every dancer seemed to remember the steps in a different way. I think I learned at least ten versions. Finally, I sat down and thought I'd just wait and see which version was really going on. At the end of a day of quarreling and wrangling, the choreographer, who himself did not remember his own work, said, "I really think it will be easier to make a new version." It is tedious to figure out the steps of a ballet from a movie, but it *is* possible. The trouble is that most of us can't afford to make movies. Let us hope that the new Association of American Dancers will help record the best of our American ballets.

We choreographers practically never have a musical score with a good scenario and pictures of costumes and scenery just handed to us. Usually a choreographer thinks up his own scenario, then chooses the composer and designer, and finally makes the dance patterns. The safest way to insure a successful ballet is to use good music that is already written, and then put an idea to the music. My theory has always been that the ballets which *live* are the ones which have a first-rate musical score, like *Swan Lake, Aurora's Wedding, Scheherazade,* and *Prince Igor.* However, to use music already written is unadventuresome, and I for one am always willing to take a chance, even if it means not going down to posterity. Or perhaps I should say even if it means going down on *my* posterity. However, I composed four of my most successful ballets to music already written: Ravel's *Bolero,* Ibert's *Gold Standard, Love Song* to music which I compiled from Shubert songs, and Mozart's *Les Petits Riens,* which I created two years ago.

I will have to admit that there are certain advantages in working with a dead composer! For one thing, when you drop out three bars of his immortal score, at least you live to tell the tale. Mr. Mozart was persuaded by Noverre, ballet master of the Paris Opéra in 1778, to write a ballet for the Paris Opéra Ballet. If Mozart would do this for Noverre, Noverre was sure he could get Mozart a real commission to compose an opera, and so paid him nothing. Mr. Noverre not only paid Mozart nothing, but himself took credit for composing Mozart's music! *Les Petits Riens* is the only ballet that Mozart ever wrote.

I didn't like the original story for this ballet, so I devised one myself to fit the music. I was able to put the ballet on in little more than a month because the music was simple and inspiring, and because I decided to use conventional tutus, and classical steps influenced by the ornate style of the eighteenth century. I had wonderful dance technicians to work with, so this ballet was a real pleasure for me. Ballet for America Company, which commissioned this ballet from me, went on the road and in a few weeks lost so much money—$70,000, I believe—that it went bankrupt. Unfortunately, I have no movie record of *Les Petits Riens*, so except for some nice notices, that is the end of that.

Usually, however, a new ballet takes at least a year to prepare. *The Bells*, which I did for the Ballet Russe de Monte Carlo last year, started off as a solo dance in which I danced and spoke the poem at the same time. I never got up the nerve to perform this dance in public, but it put all kinds of ideas in my head. I started reading everything that Poe ever wrote, and made up all kinds of fanciful scenarios which finally jelled down to the one you may have seen last year. Darius Milhaud was inspired by the idea and wrote the music actually very quickly—in about two months. The words were eliminated, because they were poetry and no commercial ballet company would have had the courage to use them.*

* The conclusion of this speech was incorporated into the following article, "Billy Sunday in the Ballet."

Billy Sunday in the Ballet

[In *Theatre Arts*, October 1947]

This season my ballet *Billy Sunday*, with music by Remi Gassmann and text by Ray Hunt, will be added to the repertory of the Ballet Russe de Monte Carlo. This is my first full-scale ballet in which spoken words are employed. The possibility of using words with dancing has always fascinated me—particularly since my first acquaintance many years ago with the plays in Japan in which the actors spoke, danced, and sang. A few seasons ago I gave a number of solo recitals composed entirely of poems which I recited as I danced; some of the poems were provided with a musical accompaniment by Lehman Engel, while others had no music at all. Even *The Bells*,

Frederic Franklin in scenes from *Billy Sunday*, Ballet Russe de Monte Carlo, 1947.

which assumed its final shape as a ballet of the traditional wordless order, first came to my mind as a subject for a solo dance-recitation.

I once bragged to Alexandra Danilova that I could speak audibly even while I was doing fancy pirouettes. This obviously failed to impress her, for she said, "And Ruth, *about what do you speak* when you do pirouettes?" If I had not been caught off guard by her candid disbelief in the whole thing, I should have tried to explain that in my ballets the dramatic effect always comes first (except in purely lyrical pieces like *Love Song* or Mozart's *Les Petits Riens*). The dramatic effect conditions or governs the choice of music and the style of movement, as well as the particular steps employed by the dancers, and similarly it also controls my decision about the use or avoidance of words.

In any ballet, however, the dancing is of far more fundamental importance than the device of using words, and I try never to let a text impair my sense of responsibility as a choreographer. My purpose is to create dance movement which will enhance the dramatic effect of the ballet *as a whole*, as well as the various scenes or parts which make it up. Since the dramatic effect is dependent upon the complete unity of music, dance movement, story elements, and words (if there are any), I let the style develop out of the basic conception of the work. I am willing to use movements employed by both modern dancers and the classicists whenever I think the work will be more effective dramtically as a result of mixing these idioms. For the same reason I sometimes allow the movement simply to come out of the bodies of the particular dancers I am directing. When I once asked George Balanchine how he did his ballets so quickly he said, "I just let the dancers do what they can do." This is of course an exaggeration, but it points up the extent to which an understanding of the special qualities of particular dancers is an important feature of successful choreography.

Billy Sunday covers as wide a dramatic range as any ballet I have ever composed. The idea has been in the back of my mind for more than five years. It began in the form of an ambitious plan to make a whole evening of danced Bible stories, almost like a Bible revue. I thought Kurt Weill the ideal composer for this, but he refused to discuss the project until I developed more of a point of view toward the materials. Some time afterward Billy Sunday popped into my mind. When I was being finished off in Miss Williams' and Miss McClellan's French School for Girls in New York, we were taken en masse to a Billy Sunday revival meeting. All of us were very much affected, perhaps more by Homer Rodeheaver with his trombone leading the congregation in "Brighten the corner where you are" than by any deep religious experience.

I remember Billy himself more as an actor than as a man of God. In my imagination, as I thought about my ballet, I could see Billy delivering a sermon on temptation, illustrating it with famous Bible stories. Fired with excitement over the whole idea, I got in touch with Mr. Weill again, and also with John LaTouche as a possible author of the text. By this time, however, Mr. Weill was at work on *Street Scene* and Mr.

103

LaTouche on *Beggar's Holiday*, and the proposal had to be dropped. A year later Remi Gassmann, then director of the Composers Concerts at the University of Chicago, told me he would like to write a ballet for me. I was delighted at the prospect, particularly since he was attracted by the Billy Sunday subject. At his suggestion we asked Ray Hunt, Sunday editor of the Chicago *Times*, to write sermon texts paralleling the style of the original ones, which we could not use on account of copyright restrictions.

In our ballet Billy's sermon on temptation consists of four stories: David and Bathsheba, Joseph and Mrs. Potiphar, the Wise and Foolish Virgins, and Samson and Delilah. All four are based upon sermons in Billy's volume, *Love Stories of the Bible*. They present a strange combination of fierce sincerity, naïveté, and good American corn. Mrs. Potiphar, for example, appeals to Joseph as "about the niftiest proposition that had come down the Egyptian pike in a good many moons." Samson's unfortunate experience shows that "steel in muscles can become as fragile as a chicken coop unless there's common sense behind the ears." I have taken the liberty of making Ku Klux Klanners of the Philistines. I do not know that Billy actually preached against the Klan, but it is the kind of evil he would have preached against.

In his revival meetings Billy often enacted the various characters in the Bible himself. In our ballet, Billy himself portrays David, Joseph, and Samson. All the other characters are played by the dancers; Billy alone speaks. In each instance he remains in his preaching clothes but puts on something to suggest the character he is portraying—a crown for David, a wig for Samson.

Some people may object to my use of toe dancing in this ballet on the ground that is not American. I have used it, however, for dramatic purposes. For example, the Wise Virgins do an American trucking step on their toes, in contrast to the Foolish Virgins, who do the same step in the popular jazzy manner. I have also put Mrs. Potiphar on her toes because she is a grand lady who is also a little silly.

I have asked Mr. Gassmann to contribute a description of his music.

In catching the local color of Billy Sunday's milieu, I chose to rely on the fact that my own American heritage included environmental influences similar to those that made such a personality possible. I naturally considered the possibility of borrowing from such obvious sources as the Rodeheaver hymns, which always formed an integral part of Billy's revivals. I decided against this, however. When you listen to the orchestral score, you will realize that Rodeheaver's instrumental fame has been perpetuated there, but you will listen in vain to find either excerpts or suggestions of anything like his hymn tunes. I did not think I could very well begin to improve on my Americanism in music, which is inevitably present since I am a middle-westerner, through conscious use of appropriate borrowings. I have sought to provide a continuous musical elaboration of his very special way of telling us some of the Bible stories in language as straight and understandable as Main Street.

The Use of the Speaking Voice with Dance Movement

[Speech given in Jacob's Pillow Dance Festival Lecture Series,
Lee, Massachusetts, August 16, 1948]

There are a great many ways to combine words with dance. The use of a narrator, with the dancers illustrating the words, is the easiest and most frequently employed and, I would say, the most successful, though probably the dullest. *Peter and the Wolf* employs a narrator, and as it is a ballet designed for children, I think the narration adds a great deal, and fits the brilliant Prokofieff score perfectly.

In Weidman's *Fables for Our Times* the dancing also illustrates the words fairly literally. But even though Weidman is a great dance satirist, I think that actually these wonderful Thurber stories are equally funny if you just read them. However, modern dancers have on the whole used their narrators imaginatively, in that the narrator wanders freely about among the dancers, instead of just standing at the side. Martha Graham tried this method rather unsuccessfully in *American Document*, I thought; but her synthesis of words and dance in *Letter to the World* was almost perfect, although personally I would have liked it even better had Martha spoken the words of Emily Dickinson herself.

In *Inquest* Doris Humphrey used Ruskin's *Sesame and Lillies* for a text. But I personally thought that the wonderful choreography for this tragedy of social protest was so clear that the words were hardly necessary.

In general, poetry lends itself to dance much more effectively than prose because both poetry and dance have a formality of design and rhythm.

Robert Breen of the speech department of Northwestern University, with his students, gave remarkable performances of all kinds of poetry, in which he clearly showed what a beautiful new idea can be achieved with dancing and speaking at the same time. He had no professional dancers, but his interrelation of words and movement seemed completely believable and natural, and enhanced and illuminated the inner meaning of the poem.

Speaking choruses can be extremely effective, but have rarely been used in ballet companies. In fact, the only one I've ever seen used in a ballet company was in Lord Berner's *Wedding Bouquet* given by the Sadler's Wells Ballet with a chorus sitting on the side reciting words of Gertrude Stein. The effect was electrifying.

(Left): Cambridge Ladies. (Right): Lucy Lake. (Below and right): Harlequinade with Bentley Stone.
Photos by Maurice Seymour.

Weidman successfully used a small speaking chorus in *On My Mother's Side*. But I thought the speaking chorus of *Carousel* added little because they seemed too static and conventional, and I said to myself, "What for?"

Sound effects have been used practically not at all in ballet companies, and vocal and instrumental self-accompaniment have also been little explored. The Spaniards, of course, shout "Olé," which certainly adds tremendously to the excitement of their climactic dances, and the Zombies in Katherine Dunham's *L'Agya* emit strange noises which enhance the weirdness of the situation. Trudi Schoop uses all kinds of oohs and ahs, and part of the effect of Kreutzberg's *Three Mad Figures* comes from the off-stage demonic laughter.

This spring I was most interested to note that in the all-American Ballet Theatre evening, the human voice was used in all four ballets—timidly and sparingly, but nevertheless there. The ballets were *Billy the Kid, Facsimile, On Stage,* and *Fall River Legend*.

We now come to the subject of ballet plays, which is my favorite theme. The first one that I know about (excluding the ancient Greek and Oriental theatres and the commedia dell'arte) is Stravinsky's *Story of the Soldier*. Can you imagine, I did it myself in 1931 and didn't even know it was a ballet play. It was performed in New York before we did it; and as they gave all the words to the narrator, we just supposed it was written that way. But it seems that both the Devil and the Soldier were supposed to speak as well as the narrator. Kreutzberg both danced and spoke as the Devil in Austria this spring. Saroyan wrote three ballet plays, one of which, *The Great American Goof*, was done by Loring for the Ballet Theatre. Saroyan should be an ideal writer for a ballet play, but this venture was not a success. Maybe it came too soon, or maybe the theatre was too big to make the words effective. The two dancers speaking the words of Lorca's *Lament for Ignacio Sanchez Mejias* in Humphrey's choreography for Limón seem exactly right and illustrate perfectly what I mean by a dance play or poem.

I think I would also call Kapek's *Insect Comedy*, as choreographed so skillfully by Hanya Holm, a dance play. Incidentally, Annabelle Lyon as a pregnant beetle was terrific, and my only criticism is that I think the butterfly people would have been much more butterfly-ish on their toes. Most choreographers seem to think that your voice leaves you once you get into toe shoes. Actually, I can visualize a sort of *Les Sylphides* done to poems of Heine—"Tears fall within mine heart as rain upon the town." Doesn't that sound like moonstruck sylphs? I hope Mr. Denham isn't in the house!

Smaller examples of words successfully used to heighten the dramatic effect are the "I hate you" at the end of the *Carousel* ballet in which Lilliom's daughter, after a long dance with the rich children during which she is snubbed, finally stops and with those three words, "I hate you," expresses so simply her pent-up feelings. A dance at the end of a long speech would have the same effect. Dorothy Bird's *If I Had a Blue Ribbon Bow* was a completely right use of words and dance combined, because the idea of those words is hard to get across without actually using the words themselves; and the way she half spoke, half sang them was utterly beguiling. The few words in Tamiris's *Tiger Lil* for Valerie Bettis were also rightly and logically used, I thought. Unfortunately, I didn't see Maslow's *Champion*, but the description I read of the relation of words and dance sounded interesting.

I feel ready and eager now to do some ballet plays on the theme of Billy Sunday, but I actually worked out a great many of my ideas a long time ago on a solo program of what I call ballet poems. I was most interested to read just the other day in Harold Acton's *Memoirs of an Aesthete* about the sixteenth century Chinese theatre (which has survived till today) called the *K'un-ch'u* in which "every pose illustrated a line of verse." So again you see, we are doing nothing new.

The poet Mark Turbyfill started working on the idea of dancers speaking and dancing poems at the same time way back in the days of the Chicago Allied Arts (1925-1928), and I worked with him on them. But he never performed any of them publicly, and I was too influenced and engrossed by the Russian ballet at that time and too young to go ahead with the idea. Then, when my partner Bentley Stone went off to war and when Catherine Littlefield and Ballet Theatre took the Chicago Opera away from us Chicagoans, I went to work on a solo program which included Turbyfill's fascinating poem, "Eros in Time of War," and other shorter more lyrical poems of the same writer, Lorca's "Death of a Spanish Bullfighter," Dillon's translation of "The Sadness of the Moon" by Baudelaire, from *Les Fleurs du Mal*, Amy Lowell and Arthur Waley's translations from the Chinese of Li Po, "Drinking Alone in the Moonlight" and "When Blossoms Fall," Sandburg's "Graves" and "Lost," Hilaire Belloc's "Precautionary Tales," lots of Ogden Nash and Dorothy Parker, MacLeish's "Nocturne," and, above all, e.e. cummings.

Like everyone else, I fall into the habit of *illustrating* the words in literal movement because that seems to be what the audience expects and reacts to. When an audience hears words, it wants meaning and will not so easily accept such strange conglomerations of seemingly meaningless sounds as Stein and cummings produce. These latter are to me ideal writers for dance and for opera too. Do you remember Stein's *Four Saints in Three Acts*? These musical words sounded just right to me for the voice. "Pigeons on the grass—alas—alas." I don't know what that means, but it does sound so lovely. As Stein often said, the most beautiful word in the English language is "cellardoor." My favorite poem to dance to is e.e. cummings's "Anyone lived in a pretty how town." But I practically never do it, because it bothers people that they don't understand it. If you think of "Anyone" as someone's name, it is fairly comprehensible, but it is the mood and music innate in the poem which I think make it so suitable for dancing.

Dance: 1923

[In *Theatre Arts Monthly*, September 1948]

Those were the days when dances were "arranged," not "choreographed," when "balletomanes" were still called "stagedoor Johnnies," and we were reading *Dance Lovers' Magazine*.

Diaghilev was having financial difficulties with his Ballet Russe in Europe, his only production of that season being the choral ballet *Les Noces* of Stravinsky. Serge Lifar had just joined his company and his three great stars, Karsavina, Lopokova, and Massine, quit.

Isadora Duncan was on her last tour of the United States, this time with her mad poet husband, Sergei Essenine. She also was having financial troubles and was denouncing America (where she felt she was never really appreciated), saying she would rather live in Russia "on black bread and vodka, then here in the best hotels." In Boston the headlines read, "Isadora Is Red Like Her Garments, Which She Removed." No headlines about her great art, but only scandals about her husband, her lack of clothing, and her Communist propaganda.

In the United States there were two touring companies which were built around the stars, Anna Pavlova and the Denishawns. The latter were barnstorming in *Feather of the Dawn* (Hopi Indian) and *Ishtar* (Babylonian), and Ted Shawn was doing a tango with Martha Graham, while Doris Humphrey was busy dancing with a hoop. Ruth St. Denis was dreaming her Oriental fantasies preparatory to her trip to the Orient, where her Hindu nautch was to become the sensation of India.

Pavlova's programs consisted of two ballets from the standard classical repertoire, followed by a series of divertissements. These included a few group numbers by the corps de ballet, one solo by Pavlova (such as her *Dying Swan* or *Dragonfly*), a solo by her partner, Laurent Novikoff (often a warrior dance with a bow and arrow or a variation of brilliantly executed batterie), the performance ending with a duet by Pavlova and her partner, such as the *Bacchanale* or the *Pavlova Gavotte* (two of her most popular numbers).

In the Broadway shows, however, the success of the dancing usually depended

Ruth Page in "The Auction" scene from the *Music Box Revue*, 1922.

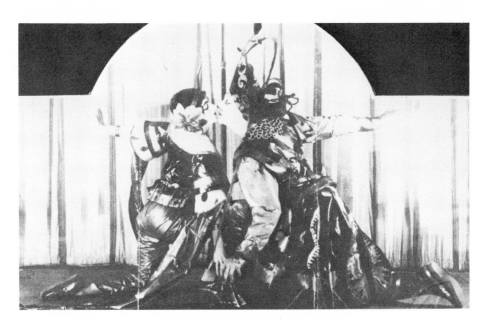

Ruth Page with Hubert Stowitts in "The Auction" scene from the *Music Box Revue*, 1922.

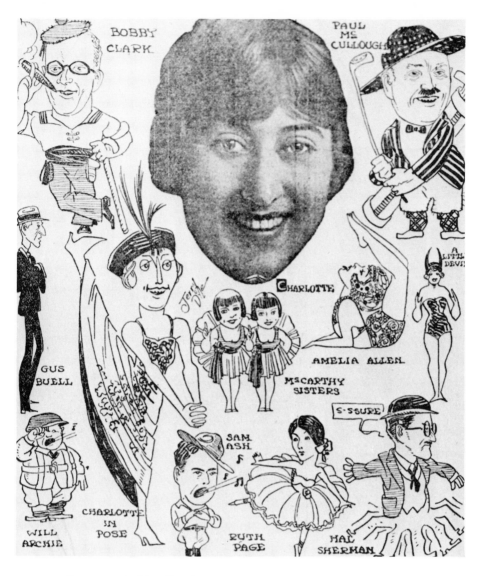

Cartoon for the *Music Box Revue* in the *Philadelphia Bulletin,* March 30, 1923.

upon the dancer's stunts. Ula Sharon would hop for what seemed like a half hour on one toe—you could shut your eyes and take a little rest and when you opened them, there was Ula still hopping. It was Harriet Hoctor, they say, who used to have such good balance that she could have lunch while still poised on one toe. The backbend was also very much in vogue—the dancer would travel backward on her toes, bending way back, and while in that position on one toe would kick the back of her head with the other. When doing pirouettes, the theory was that the dancer who kept going long enough would ultimately get a hand.

All the Broadway revues had a great deal of dancing. Hassard Short was the director of the three sensationally successful and expensive *Music Box Revues*, of which the second opened in the fall of 1923. He chose me as premiere danseuse and imported Hubert Stowitts (one of Pavlova's partners) from Europe to partner me and arrange the dances. These consisted of an exotic number called *Porcelain Maid*, in pseudo-Chinese costumes made of oilcloth by Adrian (then completely unknown), to the accompaniment of two singers dressed as porcelain dolls standing on teakwood stands. Most of the other principals danced too. Charlotte Greenwood kicked higher than anyone else, and Bobby Clark's pantomime would have rivaled the commedia dell'arte. Olivette did acrobatic comedy to "I Want to Go upon a Dancing Honeymoon," and Amelia Allen tied herself up in knots to the music of "Song of India" (jazzed).

The Roth Brothers, two beautiful figures in white tights, did acrobatic adagio in statuesque poses reminiscent of Michelangelo, William Seabury hoofed, and there was a *Hell* finale that outshimmied Gilda Gray. Hal Sherman stopped the show every night in an eccentric dance, while we classicists looked on with our noses up in our own world of cloudy tutus, without realizing what a debt some of us would one day owe choreographically to this truly American dancer. The "white ballet," called *Under the Chandelier*, arranged for me by Stowitts, was considered much too classical by Sam Harris and Irving Berlin, and was cut for the opening. But Mr. Short (to this day the champion of classicism) arranged a tryout at an Actor's Equity Benefit at the Century Theatre, where it was such a hit that it was immediately put back in the show, which ran two years.

A series of five dancers were appearing in John Murray Anderson's *Greenwich Village Follies*, including Margaret Severn (using masks for every mood), Margaret Petit, Martha Graham, Anna Ludmila (who was premiere danseuse of the Chicago Opera that fall, with Adolph Bolm as ballet master). The Astaires were dancing in *The Bunch and Judy*. Maria Gambarelli was the adored and perennial star at the Capitol Theatre. The Castles were the hit of London.*

Most of the "soubrettes" of those days had started as toe dancers. Like Marilyn Miller, Ann Pennington, and Mary Eaton, they specialized in wheels and turns. But after a season or two, they learned to sing and act as well as dance.

Of happy memory in 1923 was the then two-year-old Negro show called *Shuffle Along*, which gave midnight performances once a week where all Broadway collected. Florence Mills was in the chorus, where every eye and ear were riveted upon her carefully arranged out-of-step routines. The hit number was *I'm Just Wild About Harry*, which was our first introduction to the Negro strut. Stowitts and I took lessons from one of the boys in the show, and along with all the rest of Broadway we were strutting on top of the world in 1923.

* An obvious slip in memory by Miss Page. Vernon Castle was killed in a training flight in Texas in 1918.

114

Opera as Dance

[In *Opera News*, April 21, 1962]

A question often put to me is: What started me making ballets out of operas? There is a temptation to reply that an artist creates in a certain way simply because he feels like it, not for any logical reason. But a better explanation is that I was dissatisfied with the way operas looked, yet loved the way they sounded. When I started working at the Chicago Opera we dancers did not have a union; often we spent needless hours onstage during rehearsals, waiting to be called. I never minded spending all day and sometimes half the night listening to the operas, but I must admit that it was a strain to have to keep looking at them. So I used to close my eyes and imagine what these wonderful works would be like if the way they looked equaled the way they sounded.

My first opera-into-ballet was *Carmen*, which I adapted and choreographed for the WPA in 1937 under the title *Guns and Castanets*. Carmen is a natural candidate for ballet form because Bizet planned many of his themes after Spanish dances, as in the Seguidilla and Habanera. Roland Petit, whose *Carmen* ballet followed later, saw these same possibilities. In my version the story was transferred to Civil War Spain, with José as a Loyalist soldier and Escamillo as a Fascist aviator who fell out of the sky onto the stage during an air raid; Carmen became an ignorant café girl who neither knew nor cared which side was which. Federico García Lorca's poems were spoken from the pit to an extremely free adaptation of Bizet's music by Jerome Moross. As time has passed, I have come to stay much closer to the original opera libretto, trying to find the essence of the drama more as it was written. Isaac Van Grove, with his vast operatic and theatrical knowledge acquired as conductor and composer, has been and still is my ideal collaborator.

The second opera I made into a ballet was *Il Trovatore*, which I called *Revenge*. I had seen the opera only once, as a child; it was badly done, and my brother and I thought it hilariously funny. Composer-conductor Lehman Engel and I worked out a whole comedy version of *Il Trovatore*, and I had actually begun the choreography when, one day, I heard the opera given by the Metropolitan Opera Company over the radio. Thrilled with its almost primitive musical force and intensity, I immedi-

(Above): Roman Brooks and Lydia Abarca in Ruth Page's *Carmen* for the Dance Theatre of Harlem, 1974. Photo by Martha Swope. *(Below left):* Sonia Arova in *Camille,* 1961. Photo by Martha Swope. *(Below right):* Kenneth Johnson and Patricia Klekovic in *Carmen* (third Page version, with decor by Daydé), 1961.

116

(Above): Salome (Daughter of Herodias) with Bentley Stone as Herod, Ruth Page as Herodias and
Barbara Steele as Salome, 1954.
(Below): Susanna and the Barber with Ruth Page as Susanna center, 1954.

ately gave up the comedy idea and started to conceive the work as a dance drama based on the theme of revenge, which forms the motivation of the opera.

We performed *Revenge* first at the University of Chicago, to piano accompaniment, with costumes that were not quite right, and it was not too successful. Soon after, I restaged it for the Ballet des Champs-Elysées in Paris with the benefit of scenery and costumes by the Catalan-Parisian painter Antoni Clavé. Instead of doing just the two scheduled performances, we played it every night for the entire fall season at the Théâtre de l'Empire. Not one critic found it strange to use this typically Italian operatic music for a ballet; in fact, they all loved it. Though it lasted nearly an hour, their only complaint was that it seemed too short. The original Spanish play, from which García Gutíerrez adapted his version and from which Verdi took the story for *Trovatore*, required eight nights to perform in the fifteenth century.

The eye tires faster than the ear, so in making these adaptations the ballet must be much shorter than the opera. Besides, there never would be enough danceable music to make a whole evening out of most operas; but it is surprising how many operas do contain enchanting music for ballet. Describing his musical adaptation of *Il Trovatore* as a ballet, Van Grove wrote:

Here was a wealth of deathless songs—arias, duos, trios, *concertati*—whose definitive, closed forms could serve perfectly their dance equivalents. And most important was the revelation that these melodies were supported upon rhythmic bases whose patterns were actually dances in themselves—boleros, fandangos, tarantellas, galops and a host of other popular dances.

The great Italian had intentionally appropriated the vital, earthy rhythms of his country and Spain to add motor drive to the glorious sweep of his song and enhance the emotional impact of his drama. (The equivalent by a contemporary American Verdi would be a procedure in which the composer ventured rumbas, Charlestons, rock-and-roll beats for serious opera purposes.)

The Merry Widow was the most difficult of all the ballets I have ever choreographed. It was my husband's idea to use the music of this operetta; at first I wasn't enthusiastic about it, but I soon changed my mind, realizing it would form a perfect contrast to a tragic opera-into-ballet on the same program. Van Grove arranged the first draft of the music, Georges Wakhévitch designed the scenery and costumes, and I choreographed it for the London Festival Ballet. It was successful, but not yet the hit it is now. All summer I reworked the music with Hans May and the scenery and costumes with Rolf Gérard and Barbara Karinska. It was a long, tedious job for all of us, but finally the revised concept emerged seeming just right. The enthusiasm of some of our greatest dancers for the roles of Prince Danilo and Sonia, the widow, has given me even greater satisfaction than the public's approval.

The Barber of Seville is another particularly good example. To fifty minutes of this marvelously danceable music I added words spoken from the stage by two of the dancing characters, Susanna and Figaro. This combination worked well in small, intimate theaters; but in large gyms and auditoriums, with which we sometimes have to cope on our tours, its intimacy proved impractical. It is still one of my favorites, partly because of the beautiful and original Spanish scenery and costumes Clavé designed for it.

Another opera-into-ballet I have not been able to use for our tours is *Salome*. I created two ballet versions of this powerful opera—one very short, to the music of the "Dance of the Seven Veils"; the other, which I called *Daughter of Herodias*, to a thirty-minute version of the Strauss score. This was a particularly interesting problem, since the choreography had to preserve the mood and drama with practically no conventional dance steps. Because the difficult music was so challenging, I enjoyed this assignment best.

I tackled *Traviata* with some trepidation; so many choreographers had attempted it and failed. I thought it would never work, but the romantic spirit seemed to be there from the very beginning. Maybe it was because I went to Père Lachaise Cemetery and wept over the grave of Alphonsine Duplessis, which keeps company with the tomb of Sarah Bernhardt. And maybe it was because Marjorie Tallchief seemed born to dance the role of Camille. Most of the troupe were moved to tears when they first saw her rehearse it onstage, just in her practice clothes, under the hard white working light of the theater. Not one step had to be changed for her, and George Skibine was perfect as Armand. In our second season with *Camille*, Melissa Hayden and Kenneth Johnson proved equally exciting. On our recent tour, Sonia Arova and Patricia Klekovic had great success in *Camille*. Maria Tallchief filled in at last minute's notice one week and brought a dramatic flavor to the role which she is rarely called upon to use.

There are many other operas that I would like to re-create in ballet form. I prefer to speak of re-creating rather than adapting to emphasize that an opera should never be literally transposed, with the singers singing from the pit while the dancers enact the entire opera onstage. Leonide Massine recently tried this with *The Barber of Seville* at the international dance festival in Nervi, Italy, and despite his genius it was a disaster. The fact that Monteverdi's *Ballo delle Ingrate*, which we presented in this manner at the Chicago Lyric Opera several seasons ago, scored a success is merely the exception that proves the rule. The problem is how to transform into dance terms, which are much more abstract than songs with words, the whole meaning of the opera as a human drama, or, as Alfred Frankenstein put it in reviewing my ballet *Camille*, to "translate the libretto into the language of choreography (which is even better than translating it into English)."

The Devil at the Keyhole: A Choreographer Recounts the Times She Has Yielded to the Temptations of a Dancing Mephisto

[In *Dance Magazine*, October 1964]

"Temptation is the devil looking through the keyhole . . . Yielding is opening the door and letting him in!"

Looking back over my career, I find that the devil has posted himself at my studio keyhole a surprising number of times. And each time he's been there, I've opened the door and let him into a ballet.

My first meeting with the devil was in Stravinsky's *Story of the Soldier*. Here he was an actor-dancer. I next encountered Mr. Satan as a jazzman in Remi Gassmann's ballet *Billy Sunday*, about the life of the evangelist who wrote that warning about the devil at the keyhole. I choreographed it for Ballet Russe de Monte Carlo in 1948.

Since then, my meetings with the prince of darkness have been more classical. In Boito's opera *Mephistopheles* our Chicago Lyric Opera Ballet danced a Brocken scene of real bacchanalian fury with Boris Christoff as a powerful leader of hell.

Then came Gounod's *Faust* in 1963, a Chicago production in which Nicolai Ghiaurov made an impressive debut in this hemisphere in the role of Mephistopheles.

This opera's interpolated Walpurgis Night ballet, to music which some attribute to Delibes, is a difficult problem for the choreographer. The Bolshoi's naive, but entrancing, foolishness to this music would not be appropriate for an opera production. The Paris Opéra version is properly nineteenth century and fits the sugary music, but is extremely dull. For the Chicago Lyric production André Delfau designed ballet costumes in bejeweled decadent style which fit the period, yet gave a modern choreographer free rein.

After all this devilish experience I thought that the infernal majesty would leave me alone. But no. One day outside my keyhole I heard the devil once more calling for entry, not in the familiar basso profundo, but in a seductive soprano.

I read in *Dance Magazine* (January 1961) Walter Sorell's fascinating article about a libretto by poet Heinrich Heine, called *Dr. Faustus, a dance poem*, in which the devil is, surprisingly, a woman. Heine devised the scenario in 1847 for Benjamin Lumley,

Mephistofela with Patricia Klekovic, Kenneth Johnson and Dolores Lipinski.

director of His Majesty's Theatre in London and best known to balletomanes as the impresario who arranged the celebrated *Pas de Quatre* of 1845.

It is easy to see why Heine's ballet was not produced. Its transformation scenes were apparently too complicated even for those days when almost every great theatre boasted of stage machinery able to effect the elaborate scenic changes Victorian audiences loved so well. In Heine's scenario witches had to change themselves into coryphées, the devil with her wand changed the entire contents of a room in the twinkling of an eye, and at the end of the ballet—perfidious snake that she was—she changed into a serpent before the very eyes of the audience.

There was a lot of nonsense here, the product of a romantic imagination indulging in the most extravagant flights of fancy. Yet Heine's conception of a Mephistophela fascinated me. The poet said in his notes that he interpreted the Faust legend as a struggle between the asceticism of the Middle Ages and the sensuality of the nascent Renaissance. A beauteous she-devil could certainly be a highly danceable symbol of sensuality.

So I sent the libretto to Isaac Van Grove, my musical collaborator on several dance projects. He conceived of the idea of using music by the three nineteenth century composers who had written operas on the Faust theme. He took music for the first scene from Berlioz's *Damnation of Faust*, for the second scene from Boito's *Mephistopheles*, and for the third from Gounod's *Faust*. There was very little left of Heine's libretto when we finished our ballet, which I called *Mephistofela*, but we had an interesting new creation which the Chicago Opera Ballet performed on its 1963-1964 tour.

We have just produced a twenty-nine-minute television version of this ballet for the Repertoire Workshop Series on CBS-TV. Of course, television performances often require drastic cuts. But on the whole I think Phil Lombardo (who had never televised a ballet before) did an excellent job.

Someday I would like the opportunity of making an evening-length ballet out of Heine's complete libretto. In truth, one could go on choreographing about Faust and Mephistopheles forever and never run out of ideas. But new adventures are calling, so "get thee behind me, Satan."

Americana in the Making [1969]

What fun to think about what we used to do and why we did it! What spurred us on to look in our own backyards for the treasures hidden there? Why did we desert the swans, the bluebirds, and the fairytale princes and princesses? Well, we were young and venturesome, and we wanted to strike out on new paths. John Martin, our friend and certainly our severest critic, was there to help. I've always felt that he was himself more creative artist than cut and dried critic; he suffered the same birth pangs that we did. The period was the 1930s and early 40s, and the new dance paths we found came to be known as Americana—styles and themes particularly American.

Way back in 1925 or 1926, when I deserted my favorite city, New York, and came to Chicago as premiere danseuse of Adolph Bolm's Chicago Allied Arts, I made up a dance called *The Flapper and the Quarterback*, inspired by John Held cartoons, with music especially composed by Clarence Loomis. *Flapper* was the first of the Americana ballets that I remember.* It was cute and funny, bright and spanking new for those days. It was one of the first, maybe even the first, jazzy dance ever to be included on a serious classical program. Mr. Bolm was at first shocked by my daring subject matter, but he took a chance and put my first creation on his Chicago Allied Arts programs. He even included it on a very chic program for the Queen of Rumania. After that performance I met the queen, and she congratulated me on *Flapper*. From then on, Paul du Pont and I danced it everywhere, and always with encores.

Another of my early experiments with Americana was a ballet called *Sun Worshippers* or *Oak Street Beach*, also with music by Clarence Loomis. I don't remember much about this ballet except the Remisoff set, which used as a backdrop our popular Chicago beach with its skyscrapers coming almost to the sand. In those days, that was a novel view. I also remember doing other early Americana dances based on the

---

* *Krazy Kat* (1920) and *Skyscrapers* (1926), both with music by John Alden Carpenter, preceded *The Flapper and the Quarterback*, but did not share its successes and longevity.

The Flapper and the Quarterback with
Paul Dupont, 1926.
Photos by Eugene Hutchinson.

124

Bayou Ballads and on Gershwin's *Preludes*, but it's hard now to say how significant they were to the emerging genre.

Then, in 1933, I choreographed a ballet called *La Guiablesse*, which was based on a Martinique legend related by Lafcadio Hearn's *Two Years in the French West Indies*. I invited the black composer William Grant Still to write the music, and everyone in the company of thirty-five was black except me. The simple, poetic set by Remisoff consisted mostly of fishing poles. I can remember when I rehearsed *La Guiablesse* through one long, hot summer on Chicago's South Side, those fishing poles were very popular with all the little boys in the neighborhood. We had a hard time keeping track of the set for rehearsals. We danced *La Guiablesse* with the Chicago Symphony Orchestra for the World's Fair of 1933 at the Auditorium Theatre. Later, I was invited to stage the ballet for the Chicago Grand Opera.

In this group of black dancers were Talley Beatty and Katherine Dunham, a discovery of the poet Mark Turbyfill. During this period I was so busy working on other dances for the opera that I asked Katherine to rehearse *La Guiablesse* and to dance the leading role. She did a beautiful job! I'll never forget one special night at the opera when *La Guiablesse* was paired with *Salome*, and we were all excited because Gertrude Stein was sitting in a box seat!

Imagine in those days having an entire company of black dancers at the Opera House! It was Turbyfill's idea to form a classical ballet company for blacks in Chicago in the 1930s, and while he started teaching ballet to a number of blacks, he not only could never find the money to do it, but the time was just not yet ripe. Mark wanted Katherine to become the first black ballerina, but the idea was premature, and Katherine had started training too late to develop a real technique for classical ballet. I think *La Guiablesse* introduced Katherine to the West Indian material that later made her so famous. She also began delving into all kinds of Negro Americana. She of course became one of the greatest exponents of this type of dancing. Her husband, artist John Pratt, aided her by perfectly costuming these beautiful black dancers in her ballets.

After *La Guiablesse*, I changed to a different style with my own company. My first really big Americana ballet was *Hear Ye! Hear Ye!*, with a commissioned score by Aaron Copland. I paid him $150.00—which was hard for me to find—and he seemed delighted to get it. The Chicago Grand Opera first produced this ballet in 1934, and later when we did it in New York under Sol Hurok's management it was well reviewed. I doubt now if it was a very good ballet, but as I reread the program note, the libretto at least sounds superb:

If you don't know how fast things can move at a night club, you'll soon see. People swarm under the glittering lights. They want to be close together. Jazz bands torment the ears; pulses pound. Close together, couples dance, sit at little tables, and drink. In the glare they see things they don't want to see: Somebody close to somebody they want close to them. They feel the walls closing in. It's LIFE they want—more LIFE! Someone fires a shot—and there is less. There's murder!

And then, as you know, they have to go to the criminal court. The judge and the jurors, already so tired judging, have to judge them. The prosecuting attorney has to prosecute them, and the lawyer for the defense has to defend them. And so they find witnesses of the murder. Sometimes they find three. And, as you know, three people almost never agree. A night club hostess, who saw a dancer murdered, is bound to tell it her way. A loving couple, who saw it on their honeymoon, will tell it their way. A Negro waiter who saw it, is sure to tell it his way. The witnesses accuse three. Who is guilty? Who will pay? Can the jury believe all? Will they believe none? Guilty! Guilty! Guilty!

And in that courtroom, hearts, though broken, are beating, beating as the hammer strikes calling the next case. Hear Ye! Hear Ye!

I remember some marvelous masks that Remisoff designed for the jury, masks which resembled Aaron Copland's extraordinary face. I probably would not have remembered them any more than I remember the ballet, except that I spent the night not long ago in George Verdak's bedroom in Indianapolis (not with George, but in his bed anyway) where the masks were hung judiciously on each of the walls, making my night fantasmagoric.

My choreography for *Hear Ye! Hear Ye!* was based on what I had seen in Chicago courtrooms. For the prosecuting attorney, Mark Turbyfill, I used exaggerated, aggressive movement; for the defense attorney, Paul du Pont, I used small, satirical movements, suggesting clever, rather smart-alecky answers to the pointed fingers, fists, and lunges of his opponent. Bentley Stone and I did three pas de deux in nightclub styles, as seen through the eyes of three witnesses. For the nightclub hostess we did a sophisticated routine; for the honeymoon couple it was sweet, soft duet; and for the black waiter we did a low-down, jazzy number.

The part of the nightclub hostess, who did not have to dance at all, was played by a chic and popular society columnist for the Chicago *Tribune*, Mrs. Henry Field. She dressed in my room, and I can still smile about the way she acted. She was actually stunning on stage, where she just had to stand still, but she was a nervous wreck in the dressing room. Here I was dancing the lead role, and I had not only myself but the whole ballet to think about, and I couldn't get near the mirror! She kept asking, "How do I look? Shall I wear my hair this way or that way?" She never stopped talking and pacing up and down. I was equally nervous, but finally got to laughing so hard that I forgot all about myself.

On the same program with *Hear Ye! Hear Ye!* I did another ballet called *Gold Standard*, which had a witty score by Jacques Ibert. The ballet was American in spirit, although the music was definitely French. *Gold Standard* was a farce about two

(Above): *Hear Ye! Hear Ye!* with Mark Turbyfill, Ruth Page and Bentley Stone, 1934. Photo by Maurice Seymour. (Below): *An American Pattern* with Bentley Stone and Ruth Page, 1937. Photo by Candid Illustrators.

(Above): Ruth Page in *An American Pattern,* 1937. *(Below):* Ruth Page and Bentley Stone in *Frankie and Johnny,* 1938. Photos by Candid Illustrators.

country lovers who are just about to be married when the girl is enticed by a rich old man. Young love prevails, and the ballet ends happily with a wedding celebration, the music irreverently based on the *Lohengrin* wedding march. It was just a foolish little ballet that was fun to do. Bentley Stone and I enjoyed dancing it, and Remisoff's costumes were delicious. I choreographed this same ballet later for the Champs-Elysées company in Paris, where I gave it more of a French twist and called it *Impromptu au Bois*.

An American Pattern was my first musical collaboration with Jerome Moross. I choreographed this ballet for the Chicago Opera in 1937 and restaged it for the WPA in 1938. Bentley Stone and I danced it at the opera and then for six weeks with the WPA. I again quote the scenario because it sounds so interesting. When a choreographer dances in his own ballets, he cannot really tell whether the work is good or not—anyway, I do like the libretto:

An American Pattern shows the struggle of an individual against the standardization of organized society and the futility of the struggle. The real tragedy of this American woman is that she plunges into one thing after another in a continuous whirl of activity, in an attempt to make her life have meaning and to avoid the solidity and respectability of a patterned life. Her husband, being himself satisfied with the limitations of American business success, has little meaning for her as a woman. In her search for excitement, she seeks conventional escapes—through a gigolo, a banker, a mystic. Disillusioned by each, she is attracted finally to a military idealist whose views she attempts to share. But the violence and passion of the struggle to realize these ideals frighten and repel her, in spite of herself. In the end, she, too, must become part of the pattern, as portrayed by the three stylized matrons who are continually in the background of her life—symbols of terrifying conventionality. Her life is tragic because she has failed to find herself—her soul.

It is difficult to describe the choreography after all these years, but if I remember correctly, I was the only one on pointe in the ballet except for a cocktail party scene where the corps were also in toe shoes. The movements of the three matrons, who continually haunted the background of my life, were stiff, conventional, and foreboding. They kept giving me the implements for housework; they insisted that I return to the suburban idea of a proper housewife. Bentley Stone's choreography as the militant idealist was wildly exacting and powerful; the corps in this section did a lot of falling, running, and fighting. The choreography for the mystic was Hindu in style—sort of yoga-ish, gazing into the crystal ball hokum and not very real. The girl is impressed by everything and tries to choose a different destiny for herself, but in the end she succumbs to the American pattern. The ballet, like most of my work, was dramatic.

Early in 1938 I again collaborated with Jerome Moross, this time on *Frankie and Johnny*. The scenery for this ballet was by Clive Rickabaugh, with costumes by Paul

130

du Pont. Bentley Stone and I choreographed it and danced it every night for six weeks at Chicago's Great Northern Theatre, again with WPA backing. We did it later in New York with the Ballet Russe de Monte Carlo, and there it caused a great scandal: there were two lesbians in the ballet, three Salvation Army singers stood by Johnny's coffin drinking beer and singing bawdy songs, and finally Johnny's coffin was carried in by six tap dancers. It would probably seem quaint today, but it was immensely popular, even though "de-bawdy-ized" for Ballet Russe.

I would say that *Billy Sunday*, a ballet inspired by the sermons and style of the evangelist Billy Sunday, including spoken words taken from those sermons, was about the last major effort of my Americana period. We gave it first in a lecture demonstration in 1946 on a series at the University of Chicago, which was managed by Roger Englander. Then in 1948 Ballet Russe de Monte Carlo performed it, with Frederick Franklin speaking and dancing the role of Billy Sunday in a remarkable manner, and with Danilova as a fabulous Mrs. Potiphar speaking her lines with a real comic flair and excellent diction. However, the Remi Gassman score was not quite right for this ballet—it was too intellectual for the subject. I still wish that I could redo the ballet with the real Billy Sunday hymns and the popular music of that day.

Billy Sunday opens the ballet by preaching to the audience: "Temptation is the Devil looking through the keyhole . . . Yielding is opening the door and letting him in!" The ballet ends with: "Swing the Bat of Righteousness—Swing the Bat of Faith. Hit a home run and knock the Devil out of the box!" This was unusual subject matter for the Ballet Russe de Monte Carlo!

I patterned a great deal of the movement for Billy's role on pictures I had seen of him as the "gymnast of Jesus," and when there were not enough pictures I invented movement in his style. The role of Mrs. Potiphar was on pointe, very elegant and snooty, looking down her nose through her lorgnette. Danilova played the role to the queen's taste. Anatole Chujoy told her she was belittling herself as a great classical ballerina to play such a low comedy role, but the audience found her spicy and really laughed.

The real Mrs. Billy Sunday was horrified that I made a ballet out of her husband's life work. I tried to assure her that I was not making fun of him, that I was simply trying to make a ballet in the vernacular, just as Billy had done with Bible stories. She was never convinced.

The only other ballets I choreographed which might be considered Americana were *The Bells*, based on the poem by Edgar Allan Poe, and *Americans in Paris*, to the familiar Gershwin score. *The Bells* was given by the Ballet Russe de Monte Carlo in 1946, with music by Darius Milhaud and scenery and costumes by Isamu Noguchi. It was not really of the Americana genre, because its style was basically European, with abstract ballet mixed with a very modern movement. I danced *An American in Paris* at the Cincinnati Opera with Paul Draper in 1936 and with Bentley Stone in

Paris in 1950. In the later version the blues section was danced by three blacks, among them Talley Beatty. I didn't like this ballet much because I got so tired of the music. I do not think this score is Gershwin at his best.

I should briefly mention here a period in the American style, although perhaps not real Americana, where I spoke poems and danced them at the same time. I'm not sure how much the audience enjoyed the dancing and speaking together, but I adored doing it. For me the poems that lent themselves best to choreography were those by e.e. cummings, whose words sometimes seem meaningless, but have the sound of music with extraordinary rhythms. Lehman Engel was a gob at Fort Sheridan in those days, and he came to my home every night to work on music for these dances. He has a real feeling for words and composed some sympathetic accompaniments for me.

I am happy to have been a part of these creative years in the American dance. But, where are we going now? We've come from the fairies and the swans through mixed-media. Are we going back to the fairies and the swans or forward to some new ventures not yet conjured? It seems, doesn't it, that Jesus Christ is moving in in a big way!

Dance in Chicago
as I Have Known It [1970]

My first appearance in Chicago was at the Auditorium Theatre in Adolph Bolm's ballet adaptation of Oscar Wilde's famous story, *Birthday of the Infanta*, with music by John Alden Carpenter. I was in New York in school taking lessons every day with Bolm when he received an offer to come to Chicago. The Infanta was a little girl twelve or thirteen years of age and Mr. Bolm chose me for the part. Needless to say, I accepted with alacrity; it was a marvelous way to start a career. So I began with a great role; and when the critic Percy Hammond said I was "perfect in the role of the Infanta," I thought having a big career as a star was all too easy. Well, I have of course been going down, down, down ever since!

The picture in Chicago in those days is not very clear to me, as I stayed only to

(Above): Chicago Allied Arts production of Adolph Bolm's *Foyer de la Danse,* 1926. Ruth Page, center; little blond girl on far left is Celeste Holm. *(Below):* Ruth Page in *Birthday of the Infanta,* 1919. Costumes by Robert Edmond Jones. Photo by Daguerre Studio.

Birthday of the Infanta with Adolph Bolm and Ruth Page.

dance the Infanta and then went back to school in New York. I do know that Pavley and Oukrainsky had a large ballet company here in connection with the opera, but I can't really tell you whether it was good or not. They were rivals of Bolm, and he dismissed them as being inartistic upstarts. I remember a Persian dance that Oukrainsky did on his toes in his bare feet. I was very much impressed with this dance, but Bolm quickly informed me that it was terrible.

The next time I came to Chicago was as the dance star of Irving Berlin's *Music Box Revue*. I had a letter from a beau of mine, John Crane, to a young Chicago lawyer named Tom Fisher. Tom did not present the letter to me until the last day I was here, and then he took me to lunch at the Blackstone Hotel. I thought he was the most fascinating man I had ever met, and that day sealed my fate.

The next time I came to Chicago I was again brought by Adolph Bolm to be the premiere danseuse of the Chicago Allied Arts (nothing to do with the Zelzer concert series of the same name). This was a unique organization founded by John Alden Carpenter to produce modern ballets and modern music. Carpenter was both a businessman and an artist. Everyone had such confidence in his taste and ability that to raise money all he had to do was to pick up a telephone and call a few friends, and the money came rolling in. His wife, Rue, was a chic interior decorator. I remember with such pleasure the brilliant parties she used to give. These were glamorous days in Chicago.

Nicholas Remisoff, a refugee from Russia, was in Chicago at that time, and he became the art director of the Chicago Allied Arts. He was a truly great theatre man. He designed all my scenery and costumes from then on, and these designs were really works of art. Last year I finally gave them (at least five truckloads) to Butler University in Indianapolis. I have no idea what happened to the costumes from the Chicago Allied Arts. I was asked some time ago to revive Carpenter's *Birthday of the Infanta*. I tried to find the production in the storeroom of the Chicago Opera, but everything had completely disappeared. Robert Edmond Jones, the artist, who was one of the best designers, did the scenery and costumes for the *Birthday of the Infanta*, and they were absolutely perfect.

Tom Fisher was the secretary of the Chicago Allied Arts, and it was in 1925 that I married him. From then on I was more or less a Chicagoan. We went to Monte Carlo on our honeymoon, where I joined the Diaghilev Ballet, and he came home alone. In spite of my unorthodox behavior, our marriage was a huge success and lasted until his death in 1969. Much to Diaghilev's disgust, I did not stay with his company long, because I came to my senses and realized I could not be married to someone in Chicago and go on dancing with the Diaghilev Ballet in Europe. However, it was a great experience that I will certainly never forget.

When I came home I became the premiere danseuse and choreographer for the Ravinia Opera, and it was there that I really learned my trade. Besides choreograph-ing all the opera ballets, I danced in matinees for children. At these performances the Chicago Symphony played the first half of the program, then Louis Eckstein gave the children ice cream cones, after which came the dances. I learned a great deal from performing for these children. I remember a group dance called *Moonlight Sailing* for which Remisoff had put together some enchanting costumes that made us all look like little sailboats. I was carried away with the dreamy quality of this ballet, but practically the whole audience came backstage after the performance to tell me I had had the sailboats going backward. After that I was more careful when creating for children!

I worked hard at Ravinia and learned a great deal, as I was both choreographer and dancer and had to organize the whole dance department. I remember one day when one of the singers was ill they changed the opera from *Madame Butterfly*, for which there is no ballet at all, to *Samson and Delilah*, for which I used practically every dancer in Chicago! I spent the entire day on the telephone. At that time, my husband and I were staying at the Fishers' home in Hubbard Woods, which was like living in a country club with many people all the time. It seemed like lots of the family were always around. A friend asked one of Tom's nieces if she didn't want to be a glamorous dancer like her Aunt Ruth, and she replied, "Well, I should say not! Too much telephoning!"

From then on, I think I was connected with almost every opera company in Chicago. There were lots of changes of management, but I seemed always to remain as both choreographer and dancer. Before me, Laurent Novikoff, who had been the partner of Anna Pavlova, was the ballet master of the Chicago Opera. His company gave a few ballet evenings, the repertoire including the second act of *Swan Lake, Pas de Dix from Raymonda, Prince Igor,* and *El Amor Brujo.*

One of the most interesting experiences I ever had in Chicago was during the year of the Century of Progress in 1933. We danced *La Guiablesse* with the Chicago Symphony Orchestra and it was a great success. The director of the opera asked me to perform it at the opera the following season on the same program with *Salome.* I wanted very much to accept, but I did not feel as though I had the time to rehearse. However, Katherine Dunham said she would take this responsibility. She remembered every single detail and we put it on at the Chicago Opera with Katherine dancing the leading role. Of course, you know what has happened to her since, and after having a big career all over the world she is now artist-in-residence at the University of Southern Illinois, working there with underprivileged blacks.

Bentley Stone and I had a company together, and for many years we toured extensively and also danced here in Chicago. In 1940 we were the first American company to go to South America, and in 1950 we took our company to Paris.

During the depression the WPA had a theatre in Chicago, and Bentley and I were made dance directors of this project. For two years we had a ballet company plus a modern group. Lots of famous people were in the corps de ballet, including John Kriza and Pearl Lang. This was a marvelous two years when the government gave us the money to create new ballets. Bentley Stone and I produced our *Frankie and Johnny* in 1938 as well as my first version of *Carmen,* with designs by Katherine Dunham's husband John Pratt and scenery by Clive Rickabaugh. We performed every night for six weeks at the Great Northern Theatre and for four weeks at the Blackstone, and we had plenty of time for rehearsals. Walter Camryn also danced with us. Of course, everybody in Chicago knows about the successful Stone-Camyrn school that has been in operation for forty years. The performances given by its pupils are professional and splendid.

Chicago has sporadically had a number of interesting dance groups. Richard and Christine Ellis have had a company in connection with their school that gives both classical and modern ballets. Edna McRae and Loretta Rozak have also given interesting performances with their pupils, and modern dance has been represented by Sybil Shearer and her group. Within the past two years Chicago has had a mixed media group directed by Keith Allison and Warren Rudd which looks promising.

When the Lyric Opera started about fifteen years ago, Carol Fox asked me to be the choreographer. Up until the last year this was an interesting and happy experience for me. I think Chicago has never really realized that it did have a ballet company right here, because at the Lyric there was no mention of the company's name, nor was the name of the company mentioned when we danced the *Nutcracker* at McCormick Place. The company was called Ruth Page's Chicago Opera Ballet, and under this title we toured annually for fourteen years. Each year we danced in sixty to ninety cities. This all worked well both artisically and financially. The opera paid us for about three months in the fall; then at McCormick Place we gave eight performances at Christmas of the *Nutcracker*, which in time expanded to twenty-four performances each year. This expensive production cost $250,000, all of which was given by McCormick Place and the *Tribune*, but they ended up by making a profit on it. It took me about eight years to get it produced.

I met Ed Lee, the director of McCormick Place, at the Arnold Maremonts when he first came here. He is an extraordinary man, powerful and sympathetic at the same time. He has such tremendous problems running McCormick Place, and yet he always seems to surmount them. When he agreed to put on *Nutcracker*, I engaged Rolf Gerard to design the costumes and he engaged Sam Leve to do the scenery.

All the designs were ready after a long time and a lot of hard work, when Ed Lee was stricken with cancer, and we naturally had to give up everything. I did not think he would ever get well, but he did recover, and after about two years, when I had completely abandoned the *Nutcracker* project and had given up all hope, he called me and said he was ready to go ahead with the *Nutcracker* right away, now, this Christmas. This was in the fall of 1965 when he suggested this idea. Anyway, it is history now, and we did it. No one who has seen our lovely *Nutcracker* could say that Chicago did not have a marvelous ballet company. The dancers were about ninety per cent Chicagoans. We had great guest artists for the three star roles, the Sugar Plum Fairy, her Prince, and Drosselmeyer, but all the children and most of my dancers were from Chicago. It was a disaster for us when McCormick Place burned down. We were able to put on a reduced production of the *Nutcracker* at the opera for the next two seasons, but McCormick Place was not pleased about having their *Nutcracker* performed at the Opera House, so last year we did not do it at all, and the Philadelphia company came to the opera with their version of the *Nutcracker*.

I had to give up touring last year because I could not find a company manager, or stage manager, who really could handle the job, and the unions became so exorbitant with their touring rules that I finally gave up. Columbia Artists, our New York managers, say that we are the most popular ballet company they have ever managed. We always had return engagements everyplace, and I think they would have gone on touring with us forever. Except when the opera sponsored our all ballet evenings, we were not able to give them on our own, as we just did not have that kind of money.

When the Lyric Opera canceled its season for one year, Bob Rushford, another person who wants to start a ballet company here now, came to me and said this was our big chance and we could take over the whole season and just do ballet. I said, "Well, I would adore to do that. Have you got the money?" He said, "Oh no. It will pay for itself." Little did he know. I think it would have cost us at least a million dollars to take over the whole opera season and do ballet, so of course I had to say no. Finally, I had to abandon my company. I was extremely sorry to do this as we had it well organized, except for the company manager, stage manager, and stage hands. I had the person chosen who was to carry on after me, but the business end of it became impossible for me. My husband was the one who helped me so much in attending to all the business matters, so when he died I just had to drop everything.

Next year I will do a lecture tour with Columbia Artists of New York with just six dancers. This is not the same as having an exciting ballet company, but it is practical and interesting work. Last year my Chicago Lyric Opera dancers and I gave 40 lecture demonstrations at the public schools here in Chicago, and I found this a most rewarding experience.

For the past two years, Columbia Artists changed the name of my company from Ruth Page's Chicago Opera Ballet to Ruth Page's International Ballet, because Chicago has a bad image. In Toulon, France, the worst neighborhood is called Chicago. I was disappointed when Fritz Reiner was not able to go on the European tour planned for the Chicago Symphony Orchestra, as this would surely have helped our image.

Well, to get down to the present, there is lots of talk about starting a Chicago ballet company, even two companies. I think the idea of collaborating with Milwaukee is a good one—in fact, I think we should cooperate with all the Middle Western cities. To take a ballet company to the West Coast and the East Coast both, as we did for so many years, is difficult and expensive. There are so many big cities close together that it would be comparatively easy to make a tour every year of just the Middle Western cities.

I also had the idea of establishing a school in connection with the opera, in collaboration with Marjorie Tallchief and her husband, George Skibine, who were dancing with my company a lot at that time and anxious to make a home in America, and with Maria Tallchief, who had just come to Chicago to live. But the opera did not

138

want to take on any more responsibilities, and they were really not interested in the school idea at all.

The opera did sponsor a few all-ballet evenings which were extremely successful. When Nureyev came to this country I was able to get him for $500 a performance, so they were pleased with that. We never had the money to give many all-ballet evenings on our own. Harry Zelzer did bring us to the opera house for several of his series, but aside from that we were not able to present any big seasons of our own. A ballet season would not be half so expensive as the opera season, but still it would cost a lot of money.

So now what is the picture?

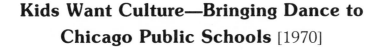

Kids Want Culture—Bringing Dance to Chicago Public Schools [1970]

One reads a lot about the public schools in Chicago and now, with seven of my top dancers—Patricia Klekovic, Kenneth Johnson, Dolores Lipinski, Orrin Kayan, Larry Long, Anna Baker, and Raya Lee—and our musical director, William Hughes, I have given lecture demonstrations in forty of them. These lectures were arranged by Gertrude Guthman and the Board of Education. These high schools are as varied as the stars in heaven and vastly more interesting to me. We had everything from complete sophistication to complete naïveté. Each school seems to reflect its principal, and I talked to as many of them as I could. They seemed to be highly dedicated people doing a difficult job with imagination and skill.

Dr. Zimmerman of Roosevelt High School made our first lecture demonstration a truly memorable occasion. How lucky the students who go to his school! The same day we performed at Von Steuben. Mr. Dolnick couldn't get the audience quieted down so that we could begin, so he just dismissed all of them. I felt very badly about it, but I really admired him for exercising such stern discipline, and in fifteen minutes we had a whole new audience. At Wells High School someone slipped in (so they say) and turned on the fire alarm, so we had to wait for the whole audience to file out and

(Above): Ruth Page and her lecture-demonstration group, 1970. Left to right: Raya Lee, Larry Long, Dolores Lipinski, Orrin Kayan, Ruth Page, Patricia Klekovic, Kenneth Johnson and Anna Baker. *(Below):* Ruth Page lecturing.

then file in again. Among the principals I met was Harry F. Yates, who has been with Lindbloem High School for twenty-five years. His face is full of deep lines and he looks harassed, but he is still there, working for his splendid cause.

The floor at Sullivan High School was so slippery that I refused to let the dancers go on. Dr. Erzinger told me just to give the lecture without the dancers. But we ended up with a very impromptu sort of happening, leaving out the pas de deux and dancing barefoot. Very unexpected things happened! Even we were surprised!

Carver High School on East 133rd Place was so far away but turned out to be one of our most pleasant experiences. We were met by Jewel McLaurin, an attractive, intelligent modern dance teacher, who escorted us immediately to a locker room where everything was perfectly arranged for us.

The most efficient backstage workers were at Spaulding—all handicapped students, and the way they got around on their crutches and in their wheelchairs was nothing short of miraculous. These students make a supersensitive audience.

Harlan High School was also extremely agreeable. We gave two performances there and had a super lunch (really much too tempting for dancers) with the teachers.

Most of the principals introduced us to the audience, and most of them seemed to want their pupils to know about "culture." I get a little tired of that word, and I think it frightens the pupils. Also, I prefer the audience of teenagers that is spontaneous and not told to behave. I like to know what they naturally react to; and, like every audience, they react most to the best. We always ended our forty-minute performance with a classical pas de deux. One young boy wrote that this classical dance was his favorite because it was so "pieceful." I must say after all the harsh bell ringing, the loud rock and roll music, so many people (too many in every school), that I myself was always glad when the peaceful pas de deux came on at the end of our program, and one could relax and enjoy the perfect symmetry and repose of classic dance.

A few of the teachers wouldn't let the boys come to the lectures and this distressed me, because I always find that the boys are just as attentive and interested as the girls. Kenneth Johnson's lifts, Orrin Kayan's beats, and Larry Long's floor exercises really impressed them. They liked Patricia Klekovic's cool purity of line (they really applauded her flawless first arabesque), Dolores Lipinski's fluid quality of movement and her warmth of communication, and they were vastly amused by Anna Baker in my surrealistic dance, *Delirious Delusions*. They liked the earthy exuberance of the spring pas de deux from *Carmina Burana*, and they even laughed at my little jokes.

The Bournonville *Flower Festival at Genzano* pas de deux, elegantly and stylishly danced by Anna Baker and Larry Long (we learned it directly from Flemming Flindt and Henning Kronstam, who were frequent guests with our company), was a little over their heads, so I tried to explain the fine points of the duet as they performed it.

I tried to teach these pupils something about theatre dance without being too pedantic about it. I showed them the difference between nineteenth century manners, where the boy gallantly kisses the girl's hand, and twentieth century manners, where a push and a slap seem more natural, and I really think they preferred the former.

What makes these lecture demonstrations difficult for the dancers are the conditions under which we have to perform and the hours. Dancers are keyed to performing at night or matinees, and if they are to start at 10:00 a.m., they have to get up at 6:00 a.m. All the high schools have auditoriums, but out of the forty we went to, only about two of them had any dressing room at all. So we had to dress in a classroom and walk through the corridors in tights, and we had to do our quick changes in the small wings. Also, the floors were almost always slippery. The more affluent companies now travel with their own floors, but it takes time and stagehands to put them down, even if you have the money to buy one. Aside from the dressing room and floor problems, we had key trouble. The room where we dressed always had to be locked, doors to the stage were always locked, the footlights were always locked, and the toilets were usually locked. By the time we had found the place to dress and the keys to unlock everything, there was little time to warm up, and to dance without being properly warmed up is exceedingly dangerous.

Our second performance was not until two or after, so we had to have lunch in the school. The food in all the schools was excellent (much better than I get at home), and everyone was hospitable and thoughtful of our comfort. After lunch we would leave and find the next school, where we went through the same routine of finding a place to park and a place to dress, trying out the floor, and unlocking all the doors. Also, the students seem to derive great pleasure in breaking glass windows, and most of the schools we went to had broken windows. In one auditorium the students had thrown paint on the house curtain and torn it, so that there was nothing left of it. In another auditorium the rain came through the roof and made so many puddles that we had to rope off almost half the stage.

In spite of all these difficulties, the response of the audience was electrifying. I think looking at our beautiful, dignified dancers takes these students into a world quite different from their mostly sordid surroundings. I like giving performances for the age group of high school students because it seems to me that this is the age that is most easily influenced. I remember when I was in high school a lecturer named John Cowper Powys came once a month as a guest to our school. He presented classic literature to us in such a dramatic way that we all read Goethe, Schiller, and anyone he talked about without a word from our regular teacher. At that age, also, one remembers everything one sees in the theatre, and this can influence your whole life. I have received wonderful letters from teachers and pupils asking us to return. One teacher wrote that in forty minutes we had done more with the pupils than they could do in five years.

Well, these lecture demonstrations should be followed up by taking the students to professional performances especially geared to their intelligence. It would certainly be a lot easier for us and a lot more attractive for them if we gave a real performance (with explanations) once a month in a regular theatre where we could perform properly. Chicago is a great wild city, and it is time that we stopped being hog butcher to the world and gangster land. We need an arts council that will do something about the image of Chicago, and the Chicago dancers really want to help. We want our lake unpolluted and we want our kids to find out that culture is more exciting than LSD.

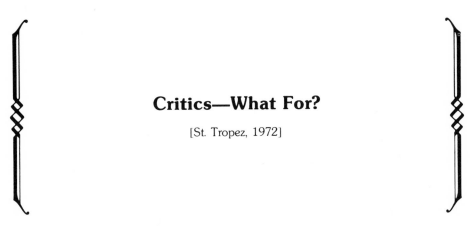

Critics—What For?

[St. Tropez, 1972]

The professional critic, he is a strange beast, and we would probably all be better off if he were banished from the theatre. While a few of them use the English language superbly, most of them are prejudiced, influenced, unfair. They tell their readers what to think, so that the public just accepts their judgment and therefore loses the fun of deciding for themselves. And most people, it seems, like to be told what they can safely enjoy.

I have had four critics in my life to whom I have listened with deference and respect, and no one of them was a critic by profession. One was an artist named Nicholas Remisoff, two were musicians, Louis Horst and Friedrich Wilckens, and one was a dancer, Harald Kreutzberg.

I met Remisoff when I came to Chicago as premiere danseuse of the Allied Arts (Adolf Bolm was the choreographic director, John Alden Carpenter was the musical adviser, and Remisoff was the artistic director). Remisoff and Soudeikin were the designers of Balieff's popular Chauve-Souris. Before Remisoff escaped from Russia he did cartoons for the famous magazine *Satiricon*. His work was always theatrical, deep, and thoughtful, but he could do "pretty" costumes too, or whatever the choreography demanded, and he rose to every occasion. I always showed him my ballets or solo dances when they were about two-thirds finished. I performed for him with fear and trembling. If he liked what I did, I was happy for weeks; if he didn't, I would discard the dance or else rework it completely. His criticism was truly constructive and I was lucky to have him at the beginning of my career.

Ruth Page and Byron Belt. 1969.

Remisoff had a short, plump, beautiful wife with great black eyes and wild gypsy hair. He loved her to distraction—in fact we all did, she was so warm and human. But she was miserable because instead of being a great actress, which she would have liked, she had to keep house and do the cooking. And what a marvelous cook—how we all enjoyed her borscht and her cutlets. The Remisoffs were friends to be loved and cherished forever. She was a good critic too. Remisoff decided whether the work had artistic value and Sophie Naoumovna decided whether it would appeal to the audience. She was very helpful.

Louis Horst was a great critic too, and while he worked with you sympathetically, he was very severe. While I was "creating" he would sit at the piano patiently repeating the phrases while reading a book or looking out into space. But when I was finished, he always had constructive comments and helpful suggestions. He had marvelous ideas for the titles of dances (he called my Bolero *Iberian Monotone*). Horst was a great figure in modern dance; I believe I was the only ballet dancer with whom he ever gave concerts. He was not only a critic in the real sense of the word,

144

but he was the most sympathetic accompanist I've ever known. His first touch of the piano keys put you into the right mood.

Harald Kreutzberg knew intuitively and instantly when a dance was "right," and no one could fool him with any fake or false emotion. I took him to a few modern dance recitals when he returned to the United States in 1965 to dance the role of Death in my *Carmina Burana* for the Chicago Lyric Opera. He was not impressed and seemed to feel that modern dance as he had known it was almost dead. Friedrich Wilckens, Kreutzberg's musical collaborator and pianist, was a cruel critic and a great help to Kreutzberg during his entire career. When we worked on dances together, we always listened to Wilckens and invariably took his advice.

But when leading music critics write a review, one feels that sometimes they don't know what they are talking about. We did Fokine's marvelous ballet in the opera *Prince Igor* at Chicago Lyric Opera in 1962. We had twelve superb male dancers for the corps (brought from all over the United States and Europe). One critic complained that we should have had twenty-four. The entire chorus was on stage, and we hardly had room for twelve dancers!

I went to a lot of trouble to get the real Fokine choreography, as I think no one could possibly do it better than Fokine. Enrique Martinez came for a week and carefully showed every step and formation correctly, and Tommy Armour sent me his notes on the *Igor* ballet. I had danced the Polovetsian maiden with Adolph Bolm and at least remembered my own part. Sonia Arova was glorious in this role and she and Boris Christoff made an unforgettable pair as he stood in the center of the stage with a falcon on his shoulder and she danced around him (before the ballet starts). Nureyev danced the chief warrior. He changed some of the Fokine choreography to make the steps more spectacular, but aside from this, Fokine's great choreography was intact.

While most of the critics appreciated my efforts, one critic said, "It looked like a Morris dance." A leading Chicago dance critic recently found Balanchine's superb *Apollo* ballet "dated, awkward, and old-fashioned." Another described the toreadors in *Carmen* (with their capes) as "generals." One can go on and on with stories like this, but these critics have the power to make or break a professional artist.

It's now the fashion for some critics to hobnob with corps de ballet dancers, go to their homes and listen to their complaints. The ones with the least talent seem to be the ones who complain the most, and I can't believe a critic would seriously listen to them.

I do not like to know critics personally, but you just can't help knowing some of them. Claudia Cassidy is my favorite "girl friend" in the world, and she is something special. My husband adored her too. Like most critics, she believes that what she says is the last word and her word is law. William Kapel used to send her a roomful of roses and then would come to her apartment and play just for her. Hurok sent her (and all the critics) tons of Russian caviar for Christmas. Do the critics like this? I guess they do. But Claudia is a fascinating woman—beautiful in a strange pale gold way, sensitive, and a great companion and friend, although she will attack her friends more severely than artists she does not know.

Claudia thinks a critic should not go to rehearsals and should know nothing about how or under what conditions a work is created. Certainly, it would seem to me better for a critic not to go to rehearsals and approach a performance with a perfectly fresh point of view. But when Claudia complained to Ninette de Valois that she did not like the English male dancers, Ninette said, "You know, Miss Cassidy, we are at war and we are lucky to have any men at all," to which Claudia replied, "So what kind of an excuse is this?"

It seems to me the background of a company has to be studied, even by a critic. How can you compare a group of dancers who have worked together since child-hood in the same school, nurtured with the greatest care and with not a financial worry in the world, to dancers who have to take jobs waiting on table (or any work they can find) so as to be able to take dancing lessons. The training has until recently been haphazard in the United States, and to me it is a miracle that any American companies exist at all. And yet America has produced some of the most interesting choreographers and dancers in the world. Just maybe this struggle to exist has even contributed to the creativity of American dance.

Anyway, Claudia writes with keen insight and poetry. Perhaps she cannot read music, and she has never had a dancing lesson, but she *knows*. If you have supper late at night with Claudia and Bill Crawford and Francis Robinson at the Algonquin, Bill and you sit silent with your mouths wide open and wonder which one spins the better yarns. Both Claudia and Francis know how to weave a spell of conversation, and I could listen forever to them trying to top each other. It is better than the fouetté competition in *Graduation Ball!*

Everyone tells me Horst Koegler is the Carabosse of the dance world, but I believe nothing I hear. I don't know how he is as a critic because I understand so little German, but as an unofficial host in Germany he was great. He arranged a supper for me at his apartment in Berlin and the conversation was delicious (the food was too). He told me everything I should see in Germany and his plans really worked—in a month I saw a great deal and was really impressed. I think if I had my life to live over again, I certainly would have opted "Deutschland über allas," because they have all the facilities, all the money, all the opportunities which we in the United States lack. If-if-if.

Walter Terry's passionate interest in the dance has never waned. He has always been a constructive friend to all of us poor struggling artists. It seems he can write a delightful book overnight, and in his books as well as in his lectures, he is most entertaining. He has an extraordinary memory which sometimes can be devastating. Walter presents dance like a showman. He is not only a real pro, he's an artist in his own right. Bless you, Walter!

John Martin is a conversationalist too. I knew him only slightly when he was eminent dance critic of *The New York Times*. He always looked like the Holy Ghost, austere and brooding, so he was a great surprise to me when he visited me in Chicago this spring and now in St. Tropez (June 1972). You can't imagine what he is like until you see him with a few brandies under his belt, an old hat sitting on the back of his head like a halo, laughing and cheerful like one of Virgil Thompson's and Gertrude Stein's "Four Saints . . ." He is full of charm and old-world courtliness. I asked my Mexican maid if she liked him and she said, "Yes, I do. He is so quiet and clean." He seems to have dabbled in everything—acting, music, painting, musicals, lots of writing, even poetry. And of course everyone knows what an inspired critic he was—willing even to change his mind if he felt he had misjudged someone. He created the dance department of the *Times* from scratch.

I wonder what you will do next, John. I can't imagine your fertile brain lying idle. I somehow think you should have been some kind of artist. You seem to have the intuitions, if not the technique to *produce* art instead of writing about it. Of course I can't say too much about you, because when you write your book about me you could very easily get even with me! John likes Scotland and all the Scandanavian countries, the cold north. He hates the sun, he hates the sea, and here I am trying to lure him to St. Tropez. Anyway, it is fun trying! I listen to every word he says and find his conversation inspiring. And what a sense of humor! I can't imagine the world without him.

PART IV.

La Vie
à
St. Tropez

I Hate You, Yves St. Laurent

[July 1971, St. Tropez]

Your blouses are always made of real silk, so they can't be washed, and they usually have lots of buttons, and one of them always falls off. Your scarves are always real silk too, and every time we wear one it has to be pressed. Even when you make a suit out of lovely cotton, it has to be ironed every time we sit down, so we really should carry an iron with us when we go out. Your colors are refined and subtle, so that we can never be flamboyant or gay, but only elegant. And how severe you are with women. Must we always look so repressed, so understated?

If you would only be kind to all of us international tramps, who must always be traveling, you would design a complete wardrobe for journeys where everything would go together and not wrinkle and would fit into one tiny suitcase. Or sell nice French maids to take care of everything, who could pack and unpack and iron and iron and iron.

Have a heart. You are the only one who always makes us women look beautiful. Now if you could make us comfortable too—*I would love you forever, Yves St. Laurent.*

Herbe Folle, St. Tropez.

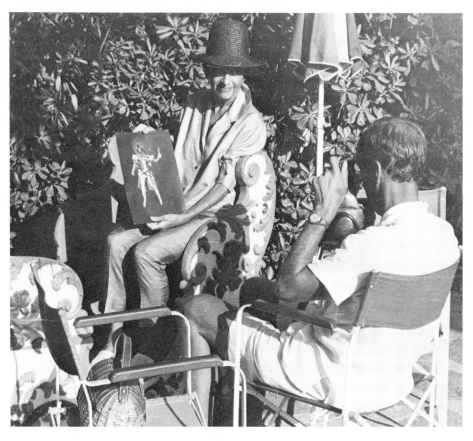

Ruth Page and Tom Fisher at St. Tropez.

St. Laurent Invades St. Tropez [1972]

The ever fascinating and energetic Yvonne de Peyerimhoff had a "cocktail" on July 6th for the opening of her St. Laurent boutique. We used to buy our summer *deshabilles* at Vachons and Choses; will St. Laurent now take over? All St. Laurent plus many creamy Parisians (Comtesse de Fleuriot, Comtesse de Sophie, Renee McCormick, Patricia Lopez) were there to celebrate the *vernissage*.

I never saw such a variety of costumes in my life. It seems that the last word in style is to wear whatever you please, and I must say this makes for fun. For over ten years in St. Tropez the ladies all wore trousers and an artistically ragged shirt, their feet bare or in simple leather sandals. At Yvonne's party there were skirts trailing the ground, shorts with lots of ruffles, straight tunic dresses above the knee. And the men were more fantastically garbed than the women.

Yvonne herself wore a bright blue and yellow brocade with earrings to match. Her dress was a long, fitted tunic with a tight skirt underneath about knee length. Susanne Lulling (directrice of Revillon Furs in Paris, and always the life of any party) wore a very long flowered silk print with lots of necklaces and scarves, all arranged in her own spectacular style. Simon, Yvonne's husband, wore a little string of a bow tie which he said came from St. Laurent, but it looked like the ties worn by the Camargue cowboys and the Spanish bullfighters. I wonder how much he paid for it at St. Laurent. Bertrand, Simon's son, wore a khaki St. Laurent blouse called *Saharienne*, which is tight-fitting and laced up the front with a loose cord. This garment is for girls and boys both. I wore St. Laurent's newest black satin outfit, and I found a couple of boys at the party in the same costume—lots of buttons and paillettes. We all wore an enormous white scarf with large black initials advertising St. Laurent. We looked elegant and comfortable at the same time. Igor Wakhevitch, son of Georges Wakhevitch (who designs so many of von Karajan's operas), wore a Russian peasant blouse (not designed by St. Laurent), a band around his long hair, and big goggles. Igor, who is only twenty years old, has just had a ballet for which he composed the avant-garde music produced at the Paris Opéra.

Victor Elmaleh, Sono Osato Elmaleh and Niko Elmaleh, with Ruth Page and Tom Fisher, 1959.

If you want to look like a girl, there are lots of short, ruffly dresses and long, flowered mother hubbards. Many of the beautiful young girls at the party had bare midriffs and were wearing chains. Yves's latest is red full trousers, a red brassiere, and a bare midriff, or you can tie a scarf around your waist if your middle is bulgy. I love the new summer dresses, very bright colors with a vividly contrasting color for a belt or sash. The trick is to tie your belt very tight at your natural waistline—it really takes a strong man to tie you into it—and for some reason these tied belts are most comfortable and very chic. If you wear a long sweater, you wear your belt around your hips! Skirts are about five inches above the knees. (I noticed in London that the English girls wear their skirts much shorter than the French girls.)

Yvonne bought her enormous old-fashioned house and garden fifteen years ago in St. Tropez for "nothing." It is in the very heart of St. Tropez, and her tiny garage facing the picturesque old Place des Lices (which has not changed) has now been transformed into the St. Laurent boutique. It is red and white with a glass front and does not look at all Tropezien.

If you want to be stylish, get out your old beads, earrings, belts, and pieces of string or go to St. Laurent.

Bardot is back in St. Tropez without Gunther Sachs and giving parties with music lasting till 6:00 a.m. Antoni Clavé has built a real hacienda on the proceeds of his Creuzevalut exhibition now in Paris, and Sempé has a new look for caricatures of St. Tropez guaranteed to keep people away from St. Tropez forever.

It's a Dog's Life [1972]

I am half beagle and half American husky, and my name is Rosebud. I am three months old, and I come from New York. My papa, Peter Brown, took me on an airplane to France. We went with John Martin, a very distinguished gentleman, and an absolutely crazy creature named Ruth Page. She sat between my dad and John Martin on the plane. *They* drank a lot and were nice and quiet all night, but *she* squirmed and kicked and carried on so that she made us all miserable. I was quiet as a mouse because Pop told me that if I moved at all they would throw me off the plane. Oh boy! Was I *quiet!*

I don't know why you have to go to France via Copenhagen, but we did. My Aunt Ruth talked so much about the Danish dancers (especially Henning and Kirsten), that I wanted to stop and see them. But no such luck. We took another plane to Zurich. I don't know why you have to go to Zurich to get to France, but we did. We climbed onto another plane and finally arrived in Nice, where we got a car. My father drives very well, but I always like to help him as much as possible because he feeds me. So I sit in his lap and tell him what to do. I wrap myself around his neck. I look out the window. I think I am very helpful but he doesn't agree with me. We drove along the Côte d'Azur, and I think this is about the doggiest place I've ever seen. You meet such fascinating creatures—all sizes and shapes—and it is, believe me, a lot of fun.

We finally arrived in St. Tropez, where my Aunt Ruth has a house called *Herbe Folle*. I soon found all the best places to take naps. I especially liked some pillows made out of old tapestry (very fragile) and of course I always like anything that is white. At first my aunt objected, but I know how to handle her. As soon as she

Rosie in St. Tropez.

scolds me I lie on my back, and this she seems to find irresistible. She is about the silliest old thing I have ever met. She calls me *Dogova Brownovitch* (I think she wants to make a ballerina out of me), and *Snooky Oukums*, and *Rosey-Posey,* and *Sugar Plummy-Wummy.* She is always kissing me, so I just kiss her right back, so we are always making love and this is not so bad. I like to bite, but she has very delicate little hands, so I just pretend that I am biting. She says I have a Mona Lisa smile; now what do you suppose *that* means?

I am in my element on the beach in front of *Herbe Folle.* There are nice soft banks of dry seaweed, and I like to roll in it and make it fly all over everything and everybody. I am absolutely the belle of the beach. As soon as I arrive, all the children call *"Rosee, Rosee,"* and I play with them. But it is still more fun to play with all the dogs. *People* always seem to greet each other by shaking hands, but dogs are much more direct and we get to the point right away by sniffing and smelling each other. I can run faster than anyone on the beach, so I run wild and jump high and *everyone* looks at me. Yes, I am already a superstar. While Brigitte Bardot lives right next door, she is getting along in years. It is *I* who represent *la nouvelle vague.*

When we go to Pampelone, there are so many people and dogs that my master keeps me on a leash. But this does not really cramp my style at all. I had a real flirtation with a great dane. He is so big and I am so little and we sniffed each other and played around together and everyone on the beach was laughing at us. We really put on a new style kind of pas de deux. Wow, did we have *fun!*

We were invited to dine one night at Antoni Clavé's—a real swell dinner. I got so excited that I vomited on a nice new rug, so my mean old aunt said I couldn't go to the Clavé parties any more. I met there a huge police dog named Poli, a very staid old fellow. I jumped all over him and really had a good time. Poli tried to look polite and long-suffering and looked down at me superciliously, but finally I was too much for him and he really got mad and let me have it. Then I saw a beeootiful cat, but I frightened her to death. I really love everybody in the whole world, and I don't know what could be wrong with me and the cats. They always run up a tree when I come around. Well, I guess you can't have everything.

We took some lovely trips. We went twice to Monte Carlo, but this place is really not quite my dish. Aunt Ruth will not let me jump on her at all when we go to Monte Carlo because she is always dressed up when we go there. We went to Jerome's for dinner at La Turbie. John Taras is with us now, and he always knows the best places to eat and drink. Aunt Ruth gave me all her *rognons*, so I thought Jerome's was really the last word and I certainly want to go back there. We went to Nureyev's house up in the mountains overlooking Monte Carlo, but they tied me up and didn't let me see much of Rudi's house, which was a big disappointment to me.

I'll go back some time when Rudi is home and I'm sure he will love me. I did not get to go to the ballet, and it was a long ride home.

Avignon was much more democratic than Monte Carlo. You can jump on anyone you want to, and this is really more my style. I could not go to the ballet about Mayakowsky (although he is my favorite poet), because everyone thought I would create a riot and nowadays it is peace at any price! But I had lunch with Roland Petit and his Ma, Karinska, Grantzeva and her *Homme du Monde*, Robert de Veyrac and Delfau at the Hotel d'Europe (we only go to the best places). We ate and drank under a shady tree till 4:30 p.m., and we really enjoyed ourselves. Everyone was so nice to me that I hated to leave Avignon, I really did. But we do so many interesting things. We went yesterday to Tallien's to see an exhibition of sculpture by Lorjou. This artist collected a lot of tree trunks and burned them. It was great for me, and I wanted to pee on each one, but every time I did it was a scandal. I had the same experience with Delfau, who is visiting us and stays in the Bird's Nest up above Aunt Ruth's studio. He paints pictures all day long and so finally I was taken up to see them. I absolutely adored them—in fact, I thought they were so great that I wanted to eat them. Now, that is the biggest compliment a dog can pay to any artist. So I ate as many as I could hold, and I have never been invited back.

I love tea time at *Herbe Folle*. I can always tell when Aunt Ruth is preparing tea, and I always run fast to the kitchen to help her. She is mad about *petits beurres*, and believe me, I share her passion. And when they are fresh and crunchy I just go crazy with delight. Right after tea we have cocktail hour at *Herbe Folle*, and we always seem to have potato chips. When they are crisp and new I love them, but most often they are soggy (like the *petits beurres*). However, I will eat anything at any time. I grabbed a butterfly the other day and ate it, and my pop said to me, "You are disgusting. Why don't you eat up the mosquitos?"

And so it goes. We have ballet class at *Herbe Folle* almost every morning. My relatives hold on to a barre and they do the funniest things you have ever seen—they are really sidesplitting. I always want to join in the fun, but they are very serious and say nothing but "No, no, no," so I have to entertain myself. I chase my tail around and around and around and I get very dizzy and intoxicated and then my bosses tell me my pirouettes are fine. What *are* they talking about?

Well, after class, it is *they* who want to play. They are trying to teach me to waltz. Now there is just one thing I just never want to be and that is a waltzing dog, so whenever someone takes my front paws in his two hands to waltz with me, I just bite and bite their fingers, and finally they have given up waltzing the dog.

They took me to cocktails at the Hotel Byblos the other day, as M. Delfau thought we should see this "monument to bad taste." Mr. Taras and Mme. Page drank six champagne cocktails with fresh crushed raspberry juice and a very stylish waiter brought me the best cup of water I've ever tasted—I was really treated royally. But after we paid our bill we didn't have enough money to have any dinner.

My Aunt Ruth gave me as a present a bright red ballet shoe. I immediately tore it to pieces. I love it because my glamorous aunt danced in it and it smells very good, just like her. I play with it every single day. There is only one toy I like better and that is an old dirty black sock that belonged to my beloved dad. He brought it all the way from New York for me (he always thinks of everything). I shake it and tear it and bite it, and I always leave it and my red shoe in the courtyard. My aunt does not mind this at all, although she says the court looks very messy, but she always puts her foot down hard when I leave my doggie-doo in the courtyard. She thinks that is just disgusting. Aren't people funny?

Last night we went to the Chapel of Ste. Anne for a ceremony celebrating the emancipation of St. Tropez on August 15, 1944, by the American paratroopers. A local band marched up the hill playing fife and drums. They were very loud and I adored them. I also adored the torchlights, but the best of all was a candlelight procession with the crowd following a statue of the Virgin, held high in the air. I tried to jump up there with her so I could see all the fun, but my old man tied me to a tree (sometimes he is really a killjoy).

Well, life is really exciting here, and every day is different. I have learned to speak excellent French (my accent is still slightly Provençal), and I hope to get invited back next summer. My Aunt Ruth didn't want me to come here at all, but now she has succumbed to my charms, and she insists that my dad and I come to visit her in Chicago. Can you imagine what Chicago will be like after the Côte d'Azur?

Whoopee!

PART V

Profiles

Our George [1975]

When I was with Diaghilev's Ballet Russe in Monte Carlo in 1925 (I was also on my honeymoon), there was a young man named Balanchivadze who danced pas de deux of his own creation with his wife, Tamara Gevergeva. Most people did not like these rather acrobatic dances, but I thought they were marvelous, so I asked him if he would choreograph something for me. I wish I could remember what I paid him, but I know it was very little—maybe George would remember?—as we had no money at all then. Anyway, he did choreograph a dance for me, and it was called *Polka Melancholique*. I'm sure I've noted all the dances I've done at one time or another, and I'm lucky enough to have found the notebook with George's dance for me in it. Here is some of it:

Run in from back left hand corner, go on toes in 5th & shake head left, rt., left, at same time lifting rt. arm from down, across face & up (4th) & then down again ending with left arm up & rt. down; then point rt. & rt. piqué, plié on left fouetté (kick), bringing rt. to back soutenu posé, then 3 soutenues on toes, rt., left, rt., then go to left, rise on toes in 5th & say how do you do with left arm, then same to rt., then walk diag. front left on toes (regular walk step) then one turn to rt. & raise arms over head. . . .

The notes may be a little cryptic, but I guess I knew what they meant, and I'm sure they prove that I must have been the first American to commission a dance from George Balanchine!

Twenty years later our paths crossed again in another Ballet Russe—Serge Denham's—when I was rehearsing *Frankie and Johnny*, choreographed by Bentley Stone and myself. George was virtually ballet master there at the time, and he watched all the rehearsals. When the pianist, Rachel Chapman, refused to play the music for the pas de deux (because she said it was impossible) it was our George who stepped in and played our rehearsals and seemed to enjoy it. What a man!

If it had not been for Lincoln Kirstein, Balanchine would probably have settled at the Paris Opéra, or someplace else in Europe. Too bad for Europe, but what luck for

George Balanchine, 1927.

us! Lincoln, in his way, is as great a man as George. My husband and I first met him a
long time ago through my husband's brother, Howard, who was a classmate of

Lincoln's at Harvard. Tom and Lincoln had a lot in common, and I loved listening to their erudite conversations on all subjects. One rarely sees Lincoln these days. Sometimes he greets you effusively and at other times he barely recognizes you. I suppose he is overwhelmed with his great thoughts. All American dancers should be grateful to you, Lincoln and George!

Ann Barzel [1974]

Ann Barzel arrives home at 7:00 p.m. and dinner for four is ready at 7:15—maybe not exactly a Cordon Bleu meal, but anyway delicious. Her icebox is always chock full of goodies, and she can get things out and prepare them faster than anyone else I've ever seen. She goes to the theatre practically every night, reviewing modern dance, ballet, movies, and drama, but going back to Ann's after the theatre is great fun. Like her icebox, Ann's apartment is chock full of goodies. While she was splicing movies I asked her if she had any books illustrated by Beni Montresor. Her bookshelves are full of treasures and there are books under her bed, in the closet, under the bookshelves, *every*place. I thought it would take her an hour to find something by Montresor, but she instantly put her hand on *The Last Savage*, the delicious story by Menotti, with beguiling illustrations by Montresor.

Ann's apartment is a place to browse in, and lucky the library that falls heir to her dance collection! Her films are of course collector's items too, but for my taste they are too fragmentary. They afford glimpses of stars that must be interesting to young dancers, but without music they are unsatisfactory and lack continuity. Why some foundation has not financed Ann Barzel, at least to the point of giving her a proper camera, I will never understand. She will go to any amount of trouble to get films. Almost all my films have had to be without music too, so while they're a help to remember the choreography, they are really only half valuable. Once, at one of the regional gatherings, I even saw Ann's films shown with music that had no connection with the dances at all. This was, to me, truly unbearable.

Not everyone has worked so selflessly and so diligently in the cause of dance. She is certainly Aficionada No. 1, and her tireless efforts should be aided by grants that

165

Ruth Page, Mark Turbyfill and Ann Barzel, 1974.

would allow her to film whole ballets with music, instead of bits and pieces. Ann has always earned her living by teaching school. If you telephone Ann at 2:00 a.m. she has not yet returned home. If you call her at 7:00 a.m. she has already left for school. On Saturdays she teaches ballet in Milwaukee, and on Sunday she teaches Sunday school. She is occupied every second. While she does her telephoning she picks the dead leaves off her plants.

Clavé [1971]

Antoni Clavé, an unusual man himself, had an unforgettable mother, whom he worshipped in true Latin style. Mme. Clavé was paralyzed so that she could not walk at all, and she would sit all day at a table painting with her left hand and singing. Maria Nieves, equally picturesque, was their devoted maid and friend who took loving care of Mme. Clavé until she died. Maria used to cook wonderful, interminable Spanish meals, and Clavé would invite his special friends to entertain his mother. I used to love to go to these feasts with my husband at the Rue Boissonade; it was all very foreign and fascinating and Spanish.

Clavé was handsome, with red cheeks, big dark eyes, shiny black hair, and a dashing moustache, which is even more noticeable now that it is completely white and his hair is still completely black. At the time I first knew him in Paris in 1951 (he was a refugée from Spain's Republican army) he was the most sought-after designer in France and I was overcome with joy when he designed my ballet *Revenge* for Les Ballets des Champs-Elysées. I can see his electrifying sets and costumes even now, especially the camp with gypsies the likes of which you have never seen before, and the tragic prison scene where the dying Azucena danced "Home to Our Mountains" so touchingly with her son Manrico. It was after we worked on this ballet that we became close friends.

Clavé painted "Femme aux Pastèques" in my Montparnasse studio, so we named our house there "Les Trois Pastèques" after this wonderful picture, which I now have in Chicago.

Clavé came with his pretty blonde Madeleine with her big blue eyes to visit us at *Herbe Folle* in St. Tropez, and soon after he bought the property just across the road from us. He became so enamoured of Cap St. Pierre that he never went back to Paris to live in his house on the Rue Chatillon. Brigitte Bardot brightened up our *petit coin* when she bought her house *La Madrargue* close by and for about three years all her fans that wanted to see their love goddess stopped at our house to ask where she

167

Ruth Page with Antoni and Madeleine Clavé at St. Tropez.

lived. Thank heaven no one asks any more, and Bardot comes here only once or twice a year, so now all is quiet.

Clavé gave up his fashionable life in the Paris theatre to devote himself entirely to painting, and now (August 1971) he has an enormous exhibit at the Palais de la Méditerranée in Nice which shows his wide range, his influences, and his change of styles over the years. As I walked in the door I was bowled over by the color, the mystery, and the enchantment of his art. How I wish he would return to the theatre! Mr. and Mrs. Herbert von Karajan (Eliette, an ex-Dior model, is a tall, exquisite blonde) also have a summer home on Cannebier Bay, and they invited us to dinner with the Clavés to try and persuade Antoni to design some operas, but without success. Clavé of course admires Karajan as a great musician who hears everything with perfection. But after hours and hours of rehearsal, he has everyone performing almost in the dark. So why make sets and costumes for them?

Now what is happening to the man Clavé? He has a big Spanish-style house overlooking Cannebier Bay with a swimming pool and two studios where he works all winter, and in the summer his house is always full of guests. He hates the chichi world and bends over backward to have simple friends in all walks of life. He loves to entertain them with the still-faithful Maria Nieves' long Spanish meals, sometimes fish caught in the bay by Madeleine and Maria Nieves from the Clavé boat (named *Maria* after his mother).

The whole band of his friends went to Nice to his *vernissage* and afterward to a charming party at L'Auberge de Père Vigon on the Corniche Fleur, and we returned to St. Tropez at 4:00 a.m. Everything starts late on the Côte d'Azur and ends late, or rather early in the morning. Clavé took me along with Madeleine and Maria Nieves last night to Les Arcs de Province, a newly restored thirteenth century town where his friend the mayor, Dr. Jauffret, organized a concert given in the chapel by Les Menestriers, a group of charming young men specializing in ancient music played on extraordinary old instruments. They ended the concert with "Twelfth Street Rag" played on these strange instruments, and I am still laughing. The old and the new really do combine to give totally new effects. Again a late party in one of the choicest ruins I've ever seen. When we returned early in the morning to St. Tropez, men were still playing boule in the Place des Lys. Boule is a serious occupation in St. Tropez.

Sometimes I wonder what effect this rather bourgeois life will have on Clavé's art. He never likes to talk about his art. Sometimes he seems almost too comfortable in his new life here. However, his nerves keep him from sleeping and he still suffers, believe me he does. And don't all artists have to suffer?

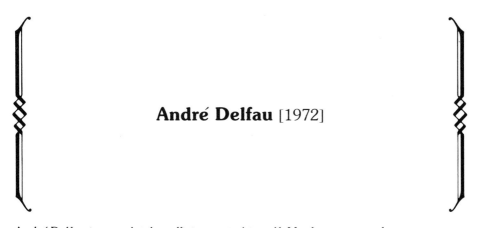

André Delfau [1972]

André Delfau is completely sufficient unto himself. He does not need you, or me, or anybody, or anything. He has great black eyes which reveal his shining soul and a diminutive stature that is very French. His private life is very private. He reads everything except newspapers and magazines. He eats a lot of Cordon Bleu meals with great pleasure, but he is equally happy on a monk's diet. He does not drink much and he adores sweets; he likes to nibble candy all day long and is never hungry. We had a long wait for something or other one day and just to make conversation I asked him what he had for lunch (he told me he had been to a very interesting, charming party). He said, "I don't know. How can you be interested in such a subject? It makes no difference."

Of course he is a person who never gives parties and doesn't understand the difficulty of making menus. He once told an English secretary of mine who was

(Above): After a performance of *Alice in Wonderland* at Jacob's Pillow, 1970. Ruth Page, André Delfau, Joyce Cuoco. *(Below):* André Delfau.

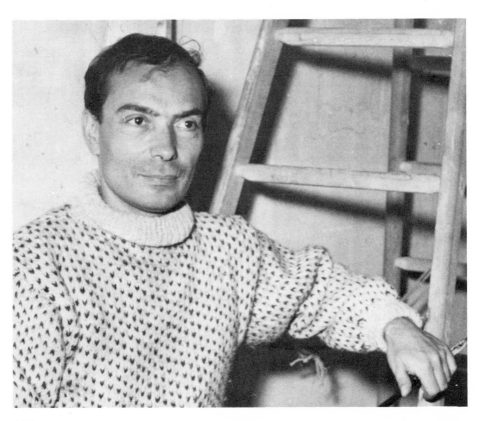

170

annoying him, "You are middle class," and this was the biggest insult he could imagine. He is antisocial, maybe too refined, and yet if you take him to a party he makes a big effort to be entertaining and always is. I enjoy his company tremendously and so do most of my friends. He knows exactly what he likes in art and the theatre, and, like the critics, he thinks he is always right. I usually agree with him—but sometimes not.

I admire Ashton's choreography tremendously. André thinks he and the whole British Royal Ballet are a bloody bore. He hates Paris and absolutely loathes Chicago. When we were in Tobago an English friend was saying dreadful things about Chicago, so I passionately told all the good things about Chicago. André did not speak to me for three days. He loves New York and London and Bombay, but mostly he hates big cities and modern life. He likes exotic places like Polynesia, Easter Island, Bali, and Morocco. These places seem to inspire him. He just finished some impressions of Bombay brothels, which he found awful but beautiful.

It is in the theatre that I have worked with Delfau. He designed my *Die Fledermaus, Bullets and Bon-Bons, Mephistofela, Pygmalion, Concertino for Three, Carmina Burana, Catulli Carmina, Chain of Fools, Carmen* (for Dance Theatre of Harlem), and my latest full-length work, *Alice in Wonderland.*

I find him an excellent collaborator. He listens carefully to your ideas and then adds his own, to be accepted or not accepted. He is a good critic and I always—or almost always—listen to what he has to say. If you really took his advice all the time, you would do nothing. He does not like to compromise, and unfortunately it is rare in the United States that you don't have to compromise.

We have a great deal in common—we laugh at the same things, we are not ambitious or pushy, and we tend to leave the world alone and go our own sweet way. His talent has not been sufficiently appreciated, although he has done the scenery and costumes for a great many ballet companies—The Royal Ballet, De-Cuevas, Harkness, Royal Danish, and so on.

I love to go shopping with him, as he can find lovely things even in a pile of trash. He leads by preference a lonely but reflective life and one of these days will probably just disappear without any fuss. I love to work with him and wish I could offer him better conditions for our creations.

Patrick Healy Kay [1970]

Patrick Healy Kay is such a perfectly charming name that I wonder why he wanted to become Anton Dolin, which sounds rather pompous and stuffy. Even with such a grand sounding name, Pat is a Dickensian character, full of Irish blarney, good company, and a thoughtful friend. I first met him in Monte Carlo, where he was one of Diaghilev's current pets. He was dancing in *Le Train Bleu*, quite a chichi ballet, but he looked very attractive in shorts and danced athletically. Later I saw him in London performing brilliantly in a rather corny old-fashioned pantomime which I adored.

Pat really did a little of everything. He was a smart businessman as well as a good artist, and he always did whatever was necessary for his career. He is an excellent comedian (and was funny and right for Baron Popoff in my *Merry Widow*) as well as a splendid romantic partner. He and Markova were exciting together in *Giselle*—quite unforgettable. He is not an original choreographer at all, but he probably stages *Giselle* as well as anyone in the world, and his *Pas de Quatre* is a hit everywhere. He takes ideas and steps from everywhere and uses them as his own. And why not?

Unlike most dancers, Dolin is gregarious. Wherever he is, he knows *everyone*, and unlike most dancers he is at home with all kinds of people (especially rich ones). I had such an enjoyable trip with him to Montreal, and he arranged a private seance with Pierre Trudeau and took me with him. I was certainly impressed with the prime minister, especially when, after a performance of Les Grands Ballets Canadiens, he came backstage, sat on the floor with the dancers, and entertained us with yoga exercises. I wrote about this to our Mayor Daley of Chicago, suggesting that he do the same, but I am afraid our esteemed mayor is more at home with politicos than with ballerinas.

I invited Dolin to dance the role of Drosselmeyer in my production of the *Nutcracker* at McCormick Place in Chicago. He was perfect in the part and did all the magic tricks I gave him with real humor. His acting and his rapport with our children

Anton Dolin in Ruth Page's *The Nutcracker*, 1970.

kept the first act lively, and I have looked forward to his appearance with us every year.

Dolin can be a sly fox too. He somehow succeeded in bringing a beautiful young male dancer named Igor out of Yugoslavia. He hired a car and a chauffeur and brought Igor to St. Tropez to see me. I certainly was impressed. So was Kirsten Simone. She and Dolin came to Chicago to dance in my *Nutcracker* according to contract. Shortly after, Igor arrived, and I really couldn't tell who had the greater success with this boy—Kirsten or Pat.

I think Dolin would love to have a title. No one would appreciate it or use it more. I do hope you get it, my beloved darling Pat.

Flemming Flindt—Family Man [1973]

Imagine—Flemming Flindt has become a family man! I knew him in his carefree dancing days in France, when he was living with Josette Amiel and they both danced at the Paris Opéra. They were lively and joyous and seemed so happy in each other's company. They came on tour with my company in the United States. These Columbia Artists-managed tours took us to six cities a week, and we traveled by bus. Flindt and Amiel danced in my *Merry Widow* and the Bournonville *Flower Festival Pas de Deux*. They also danced many performances of our Chicago *Nutcracker* at McCormick Place. Flemming staged his ballet *The Lesson* for us and we took this one season on tour with Amiel but without Flemming. It proved too complicated a ballet for one night stands, so on later tours we did it only in big cities. It is a very effective ballet, but the scenery is just too big for touring.

I saw Josette in St. Tropez sometimes in the summer, but I had completely lost track of Flemming. He returned to Copenhagen to direct the Royal Danish Ballet, and Josette is freelancing. It seems that Flemming is doing a good job. I was in Copenhagen for only three days, but I saw three performances and watched a number of classes. His staging of *Fledermaus* is very balletic and certainly very amusing with lots and lots of dancing, even by the singers. It is much too long, but

174

Flemming Flindt and Josette Amiel in Flindt's *The Lesson*.

full of clever tricks and is a big hit. His *Triumph of Death* is a masterpiece of staging—not at all balletic, but interesting from beginning to end. The Ionesco play *Jeu de Massacres* was not a success in Paris, but as a ballet it has been given in Copenhagen seventy-five times to sold-out houses. Flindt's *Nutcracker* I liked much less. Clara was a big girl and a ballerina—but she acted like a child. Knowing what good dancing actors the Danes are, I had expected more. However, it was a cozy piece, and the audience seemed pleased with it.

Flindt's class for boys between the ages of twelve and fifteen, which he gives every morning at 8:45, is interesting to watch. There is certainly nothing sissy about this class. All the boys have to take gymnastics, and they look like real, natural, rowdy boys and have trouble pointing their toes, just like little boys everywhere. Henning Kronstam's class for the older boys is virile too. The day I watched this class, John Percival, the English critic, was there and the boys really knocked themselves out, but maybe they do that anyway.

At last I met Vivi, Flemming's wife, and she is really something! She has a smile that seems to stretch from here to eternity and she exudes *joie de vivre*. At the Flindt's home after the performance, their four-year-old Bernadette was the star of the party. Flemming confessed to me that he was madly in love with her, and no wonder. John Percival was at the party and he seemed deeply interested in the Danish ballet's spring season at the London Coliseum. That evening I met Tom O'Horgan for the first time. He comes from Oak Park, Illinois, and I live in Chicago, but we had never met until Copenhagen. He finds producing much easier there than in America. Flemming says it is an ideal place to work.

Certainly working conditions for the ballet are superb and there seems to be nothing of interest going on at all in the winter in Copenhagen, to seduce you away from your work. Lunching with Vera Volkova, I was told more or less the same thing by her—she enjoys her work, but says life in the city is dull and the climate terrible.

Having supper with Kirsten Simone, who is still perfectly beautiful, I gathered she would like to guest as much as possible since she dances little, as Flemming wouldn't make Igor (her boyfriend) a soloist, so he left for Germany. Kirsten's brother is a neat technician, but he has a wife and two children and it would be difficult for him to leave. In fact, the whole ballet refuses to tour. One month in New York and the Kennedy Center in Washington and one week in London is more than enough for them.

Their corps de ballet salaries (about $10,000 a year) seem great to us, but they have sixty percent taken for taxes. The soloists get little more than the corps and are now listed alphabetically. Still, they can retire as early as thirty-five and get a pension, and they almost all seem to lead normal family lives. And Flemming, after his salad days on tour, is settled down with a family and an entire company to direct—a family man, at last!

Marigoula [1970]

Almost everyone in the world has heard of Margot Fonteyn and almost everyone in the world loves her.

My husband and I were sitting in a swing in the garden of the Fonte Napoleoni in Elba in 1951. We had sent a telegram to Trudy Goth saying that we were coming to the island to visit her, but she never received the telegram, and we couldn't find her, so we went to the hotel. A beautiful girl kept walking back and forth in front of us, and finally she came up to me and said, "Aren't you Ruth Page?" I said, "Why yes, I guess I am," and it was at that moment that our long friendship started. I never did find out what Margot was doing in Elba, but she certainly seemed glad to find a couple of pals.

The following year we went to Athens together, and Frederick Ashton and John Craxton came along. My husband found the only boat in the harbor that was for rent (this was before the tourist rush to the Greek Islands). Margot found a couple of friends in a cafe, Patrick Leigh Fermor (Paddy) and Joan Rainer, and off we went for a month in the *Eliki*. John Craxton had just designed *Daphnis and Chloë* for the Royal Ballet and had laid the scene in modern Greece. Fermor had written a number of books on Greece, his latest one being about the isolated Mani peninsula, and Joan Rainer took photographs to illustrate his books. They were a rather strange and fantastic couple. They seemed to adore each other, but I think his rugged austere life was sometimes hard on her, and she liked to go back to England where she was a great favorite with the men in London's literary circle.

Anyway, there were seven of us in the adventurous group, ready for anything. Paddy told our captain where to go, and we went to all kinds of islands where no tourist had ever set foot. We usually had a donkey for Margot and sometimes for Freddy and me, but mostly we walked and climbed and swam all day, then slept at night on the ship. Paddy and John both spoke Greek, which was a great help on the small islands. We rarely talked about dancing, although Tom loved all my dancing friends (especially Margot), and after a few years of living with me and my entourage, he talked more intelligently about ballet than I ever could.

(Above): Margot Fonteyn doing a barre aboard the "Eliki," 1951. (Below): Ruth Page and
Margot Fonteyn in Greece, 1951.
(Right): Margot Fonteyn and Frederick Ashton doing a barre aboard the "Eliki," 1951.

The *Eliki* was not exactly what you would call a swank yacht. In fact it wasn't a pleasure craft at all, just a nice big fishing boat. There was only one toilet, which was just off Tom's and my cabin. It usually didn't work, and everyone had to go through our room to get there, and the smell would have been a little too much, had we not imbibed a good deal of ouzo and retsina. At this time, Margot and I started calling each other by our Greek names. She was Marigoula and I was Ruthaki, and we still use these names.

We had spent about three weeks wandering around the islands when we got into a terrifying storm; the anger of Poseidon seemed bent on destroying us. Everyone was very brave except Freddy and me, and we clung to each other, fearing a watery death in the Aegean Sea. We finally found shelter in a little harbor, where we abandoned the *Eliki* and reached shore, soaked but safe. There was only one house in this port, and I will never forget the hospitality of these fine peasants, who fed us and gave us dry clothes and then sang and danced for us.

Margot had to be in London for a performance at Covent Garden, and it was Tom's job to get her there. Like the efficient organizer that he could be, he somehow gathered together seven donkeys and a guide, and we all rode across the entire island and found on the other side a regular passenger ship that brought us back to Athens. It was rather an ignominious ending for such an imaginative trip, but Marigoula reached London in time for her performance.

We all had such a friendly time together that the next summer we decided to go to Italy and spend a month at the Villa Cimbrone in Rapallo. The villa, built by Lord Grimthorpe in the nineteenth century, was lovely, spacious, and comfortable, its greatest claim to fame being that Greta Garbo and Leopold Stokowski had lived there together. There was no road at all leading to it, only a narrow footpath for about three blocks. But when you arrived the view over the mountains and sea was overwhelming, the gardens were romantic, and it was peaceful not to be on a highway. I hope no one has changed it.

The English really like to eat when they go on a holiday. We used to go to the beach every day with a picnic. I told the cook just to give us cheese and fruit and wine, an American style lunch. But our English friends balked at this. They wanted hors d'oeuvres, chicken, salad, ice cream, and all the trimmings. We came back to the villa about 4:00 p.m., had a real English high tea with lots of conversation, and at 10:00 p.m., we ate a big dinner. So we lived Italian style and loved it.

Donald Albery, Margot's friend and business adviser, came down to Rapallo from London to see if she was getting along allright, as I think he was suspicious of her wild American friends. He was a rather crotchety Englishman, extremely successful in producing all kinds of theatre ventures. He was even director of the London Festival Ballet for a while. He was fun in a kind of brusque way. I had dinner at his home in London one night. He had just returned from Paris, where he had been to a *solde* at Dior's. He wanted to bring his lovely wife a Dior dress. There was only one left and he bought it. He said, "Well, I figured the worst dress in the collection would be better than the finest dress in any other collection."

I was always curious to see Massine's island (L'île des Sirenes), just off the coast of Positano. We hired a little boat and with Margot and Freddy took our picnic and arrived at the dock about lunchtime. No one was there so we got off the boat and had a nice quiet lunch on the pier. The island seemed absolutely deserted. We walked all over the enormous rocks and finally got up the nerve to enter the big house. We tiptoed all over it and finally found Massine fast asleep in his bed with his arms crossed over his chest, looking ascetic and severe but beautiful in this calm state of sleep. I always loved Massine's looks—those big, serious eyes and his small, pale face.

We giggled a bit, then tiptoed out, leaving a note by his bed. We got to our boat and chugged out to sea, then we saw Mme. Massine rushing to the pier, waving for us to come back. Margot and Freddy wanted to see the island, but did not especially want to see the Massines. They both like to get away from the ballet on their holidays (I'm surprised they put up with such an aficionado as me), so we didn't go back.

We had a party later at Cimbrone to which all the Massines came, and so did Virginia Donaldson. She whispered to me to please send her some kind of telegram saying she had to leave the island. She said she felt trapped and isolated there and couldn't find a good excuse to leave. I thought the island dramatic and rugged, and I think Massine's idea to build a theatre and have a dance festival there would be difficult but exciting.

Marigoula had an adorable walkup apartment in London near Covent Garden in the flower market district. It had lots of tiny rooms and lots of pretty little things in it. I adored this place and stayed with Margot there while I rehearsed my ballet *Revenge* with the Ballet des Champs-Elysées company, which was then performing in London. These were Margot's bachelor days, and of course everything changed when she married Tito de Arias.

Tito was *the* man in Margot's life. Tom and I first met him at a lunch party at Paul Louis Valère's on the south coast of France. Tito was not interested in ballet or the ballet world, and Margot is one of the few dancers I have ever met who could completely divorce herself from dance when she was with other people. Almost everyone was French at this party and I think Tito was glad to have Tom to talk to. They spoke the same language in more ways than just English. Tito is a man of the world with strong political ties in Panama, where his family is very important. Margot's mother is Brazilian (her father English), and I think Margot felt at home in the Latin-American atmosphere of Panama.

Margot looks like her mother, the black queen as everyone calls her. Mr. and

Mrs. Hookham with their daughter were living in China when Margot, at an early age, showed talent, and her mother decided to take her to London to study. This was of course essential to Margot's career, but it was not so good for her mother's marriage. When the black queen decided to return to her husband, the story goes that he already had someone else. I don't know if this story is true, but it is true that many sacrifices have to be made for a career!

As Mrs. Arias, Margot Fonteyn was a lovely ambassadress from Panama in London, and she entertained gracefully in her new London house. I suppose everyone knows the story of how Tito was shot while visiting his family in Panama. He and Margot were reported as trying to start a revolution, but I never heard the truth about this story, and Panamanian politics is too complicated for me. Anyway, Tito was paralyzed and hovered between life and death for a long time. Margot of course behaved like the saint that she is, staying by his side at the hospital and having her career at the same time. How many people do you know who could lead this double life?

Now Tito gets around in a wheelchair, but he can't walk at all and can barely talk. They came to see us in St. Tropez in Sam Spiegel's yacht not too long ago. Margot had hoped Tito could get off the ship, but it just wasn't possible. However, Tito loves to travel and be a part of Margot's life. I went to see her dance in *Carmina Burana* in Dallas this winter (1970), and Tito was there. He came to the Kingsbury sisters' party after the performance and seemed to enjoy himself as Margot fed him.

The *Carmina* performance started with all the artists strolling around in the audience—even Margot in a blonde wig holding the hand of a little black child. All the artists wore whatever they wanted—Santa Claus, Robin Hood, baton twirlers, Sally Rand, opera costumes, just any old thing. *Carmina*, directed by Bertrand Castelli and George Skibine, seemed to be an attempt to stage this work in the manner of *Hair*, anything-goes style. It was pretty silly (although the audience liked it), and Margot's talents were wasted. What a good sport she is!

Like Nureyev, Fonteyn has turned into a social lion and takes that in her stride too. Tom and I had a party for her and the whole Royal Ballet on their first visit to Chicago. The English are always so polite, and Margot is the soul of graciousness even after a long, hard performance. I don't know how they do it. As I know how starved dancers are after a performance, I had all the dancers eat before the other guests. This made a big hit with the performers. I have suffered through so many after-the-theatre parties on tour where we had lemonade and cookies instead of the steak and red wine we needed. I finally got to the point where I didn't accept invitations to parties until I found out what they would give us to eat!

Maria Tallchief and Buzz Paschen (her charming husband) and I had a party for Margot and Rudi on their last visit to Chicago. Most of the boys from the ballet wore fancy ruffled shirts, Victorian style, and they looked very elegant indeed. I had seen them a few summers earlier on the beach at St. Tropez, where they looked quite different. I was strolling along the nudist beach (very much overdressed in a tiny bikini), thinking how ugly everyone looked, when I spotted a group of boys completely naked. They looked like young Greek Gods, so I walked a little closer to get a better view. They started waving and calling, "Hello, Ruth!" Here they were, the Royal Ballet boys in the nude, and they looked great! But I liked them in their Victorian frills too!

Sybil Burton was in Chicago the day of our party, and although I had never met her, she telephoned and said she would like to come. She turned out to be the life of the party and I should think Richard Burton would have had a hard time choosing between her and Liz. Rudi brought Lee Radziwill to the party. She dresses so well that it is pleasure just to look at her. Margot, too, loves clothes and always looks like a model of the very latest styles.

I have never had the opportunity to work with Fonteyn; ours has been a different kind of relationship. I can't imagine anything better than seeing her in some of my ballets, but somehow the occasion has never presented itself, and I regret it deeply.

I hope she will dance forever. She is a very special person and I, along with everyone else, love her deeply.

[Later: April 5, 1972]

Just returned from the new island of Great Harbor Cay, where Margot and Tito Arias are building a house. I met them in Palm Beach where Fonteyn danced at a benefit arranged by Mary Howes to raise money to build a new theatre in Palm Beach. At $100 a ticket, it was naturally a very swank audience, with a nice party afterward.

Was glad to see Carole Mandel, who looked as beautiful as ever, but she reported that Leon is very ill. The Al Stephenses gave a great party for 250 people just before the ballet in their fancy, enchanting, enormous house. The next day I went with Margot and Tito in a private plane to the new island. We had a charming lady pilot who scared me to death. David Wall (Margot's new partner from the Royal Ballet) and David Weston (Douglas Fairbanks' son-in-law, who is building Margot's new house) took turns sitting with her in the cockpit. She was always looking at and talking to these two charming men, and I felt like telling her to keep her eyes on the road, but I don't know how to say it when you are in the air, and what does the pilot keep his eyes on?

Anyway, we arrived and stayed at one of the so-called town houses built for people with yachts. Margot has an entrancing little beach where I went wading all alone. The tide was low and I walked way out, picking up lovely little pebbles and things, when all of a sudden I almost disappeared in some quicksand. I somehow pulled myself out, and later we went swimming on the regular beach, which seemed to have no hazards. Great Harbor is just beginning to be developed, and maybe it is nicer now than it will be—just a few houses, only two telephones on the whole island, a marvelous golf course, a few palm trees that have to be propped up, and lots of deserted beach.

Margot wants me to buy a lot right next to hers, but I somehow think I prefer St. Tropez with all its drawbacks. We left the island by the regular plane. When I arrived in Miami I immediately caught a plane to Chicago, and Margot and Tito went on to London. When I arrived home at 10:30 p.m. I found Virginia Johnson and Paul Russell of the Dance Theatre of Harlem rehearsing in my studio, so I took off my hat and worked with them until 1:00 a.m. They were rehearsing for my ballet on May 12th and I think they are terrific. They stayed with me and were delightful guests.

Freddie Franklin: "God's Gift to Choreographers" [1976]

Is Freddie Franklin as ebullient as he always seems? The answer is yes! He was apparently born that way. When any choreographer starts a new ballet with Freddie, he gives his all. He is always with you or even a step ahead, and sometimes quite mediocre ballets will be a success on account of his immediate rapport with the audience. Critics often said he was a blond with a dark personality, and his vitality and diversity certainly reveal the depth of his personality. When he danced and acted the part of *Billy Sunday*, he had never spoken and danced at the same time. He doubted nothing, and he, along with Danilova, who also spoke and danced, made an indelible impression as comedic actors.

Freddie is also blessed with a photographic memory. He can stage ballets quicker than anyone else in the world, and they always come off with great flair and polish. Our *Sleeping Beauty Act III*, danced by the Chicago Ballet, which he co-directs with me, was a result of his inspiring direction and coaching. Our dancers looked sensational!

Some people say that such boundless enthusiasm must be superficial, but knowing Freddie as long as I have, I totally disagree. Freddie doesn't like disagreeable responsibility of an unartistic nature, but what artist does. I love working with him. Bless you, Freddie!

(Above): Ruth Page, Andrew Wentink and Frederic Franklin in Ruth Page's home in Chicago, 1978. *(Below):* Frederic Franklin and Kirk Peterson with Ruth Page, 1978.

Kreutzberg as I Remember Him

[In *Dance Magazine*, August 1968]

If ever an angel walked this earth, it was Harald Kreutzberg. Anyone who ever came under the spell of his celestial dances, the *Angel of the Annunciation*, so delicate and truly spiritual, or his *Angel of the Last Judgment*, so powerful and meaningful, will know what I mean. But Harald could evoke any mood in his great dancing. His rapport with any audience, any place, was immediate and overwhelming. He could make his public laugh or cry at will.

I was privileged to have been his partner off and on for five years, and it was the happiest time in my life. I have worked with lots of great artists, but never anyone like Harald. He was a law unto himself. His beautiful hands, his exquisite profile, the way he walked, the way he ran—he could express any nuance of emotion with the greatest economy of movement. And his instinct always seemed right. He also sensed immediately when other artists in any field were faking emotions.

Dancing with Kreutzberg was like dancing with a disembodied spirit—the spirit of dance itself. Even doing a piece of choreography together seemed a natural thing. We just worked it out. I believe his long-time partner, the fascinating Yvonne Georgi, worked that way with him too. Friedrich Wilckens, his pianist and great friend, contributed in a very important way. He not only composed the music for Harald's dances, but would sit quietly at the piano during the rehearsal period, interrupting only when we seemed to get stuck or when we couldn't quite make a decision. Louis Horst used to be wonderfully helpful in the same sort of understanding way.

Harald hated chichi and chic. He preferred to be alone rather than with people who didn't seem to be real. He had few close friends, but to those few he was a source of unending delight. He was like an animal in that he dearly loved to eat and sleep as well as to move. And how he loved to laugh! When we were performing in Japan we often went to the Japanese theatre, which we both enjoyed enormously. Afterward, Harald would entertain Wilckens and me with imitations of the Japanese actors. And he was devastatingly accurate.

186

We had so much fun touring together. We danced in one little town in the Rocky Mountains where we did a program of duo and solo dances. It was avant-garde for those days, and the only kind of program we had. We danced a bacchanale together, our faces bound up with elastic bands. We executed all kinds of falls and got up dozens of times—it was killing and very new at the time. The program also included Harald's solo *Revolt*, his captivating *Hungarian Dance* (which wasn't Hungarian at all), his noble *Master of Ceremonies, Till Eulenspiegel*, and his angel dances, and I (being in my sack, mask, and stick period) danced *Expanding Universe* in a Noguchi sack, *Variations on Euclid* with long elastic bands and sticks, *Tropic* (all on the floor, which was considered ever so daring at that time), and Casella's *Humoresques*. The next day there was a long article on the front page of the local newspaper saying how unusual and great our program was—the praise was ecstatic, but it ended, nevertheless, with "We hope they never come back." We laughed and laughed.

A few years ago my husband and I were motoring from Italy to Bayreuth and Harald came from Vienna to meet us in the fascinating town of Lindau on an island in Lake Constance. We were having a drink in the soft open air of a second-floor bar overlooking the harbor, which was guarded by a huge stone lion looking seaward. Harald surprised us by laughingly telling how the lion had been modeled from the one which the Burgomaster had borrowed from his father's circus, years before he brought it to Philadephia where Harald was born. My husband's response was typical: "Harald, did you see the lion turn around and wink at us just as you ended your story?" Harald's reply was equally typical: "He always does," he said.

The last time I saw Harald was in Chicago about three years ago, when he came to dance the role of Death in *Carmina Burana* at the Chicago Lyric Opera. Joseph Witt of the Vienna Opera directed so feelingly, so right for *Carmina*. I did the choreography, and our collaboration was completely sympathetic. Harald had naturally changed a great deal with the passage of time, and my young dancers couldn't understand why everyone had been so thrilled with his dancing. His body had become heavy and he could no longer move freely. But he still had the extraordinary masklike face, which made him ideal for the Death figure.

I thought he would be interested to see the new generation of modern dancers, and indeed he was. But when I took him to three concerts of three different groups of the top echelon of modern dancers, he was not impressed. He thought most of their dances seemed contrived, searching for novelty for its own sake, and he was not moved.

He spent his last years in a snug house in the Austrian Tyrol (pictures of which appeared in the May 1958 issue of *Dance Magazine*), a charming house with much evidence of his taste and talent. He taught ten days a month in his Swiss studio in

Harald Kreutzberg, Ruth Page and Friedrich Wilckens on shipboard to Japan, 1934.

(Above): Harald Kreutzberg. (Below): Harald Kreutzberg and Ruth Page aboard ship.

Harald Kreutzberg in the Chicago Lyric Opera production of *Carmina Burana,* with choreography by Ruth Page, 1965.

Bern. Like him, his classes were unique and inspiring, mostly because one never got over the pleasure of seeing him demonstrate.

Goodbye, dear Harald. I'm sure no angel in heaven will ever be as beautiful as you were on this earth.

Alicia Markova [1971]

I first met Alicia Markova (*née* Marks) in Monte Carlo in 1925. She had just joined the Diaghilev Ballet, and I was on my honeymoon. She was tiny, with spindly legs, a birdlike face with great dark eyes, and none of the bravura style that we associate with ballerinas today. Diaghilev believed completely in Cecchetti training, and everyone in the company had to take his classes. Markova, Vincenzo Celli, Chester Hale, and I had a class all to ourselves every morning (while my husband rowed on the Monegasque crew). The Diaghilev company was always rehearsing in the large studio (I saw this studio again last year, and it did not seem big at all), so we had our lessons in a very small studio just next door. I will never forget these tough lessons. We all worshipped Cecchetti, even though he made life hard for us. He never demonstrated the steps, but just sat there in his chair with a cane beating time and singing. If we ever did anything wrong, he would get up in a rage and throw the cane at us. Diaghilev came to watch our class one day, and after the class he asked me if I would join his company, which flattered me beyond words as he had never before invited an American girl.

Markova, since her Diaghilev days, has had a great career all over the world, and with that strange little body of hers she has produced all kinds of wonders. She specialized in classical roles. No one would ever think of casting her as the *Merry Widow*. She was the complete antithesis of everything that one expects from the alluring, voluptuous widow of Franz Lehar's operetta. Hassard Short, the great Broadway director, who was working with me on the *Widow*, thought she could do it, and so did I. We had already redone the whole musical score with Hans May, as I had choreographed a less complete version of the *Merry Widow* for the London

Alicia Markova in *Merry Widow*, 1955. Photo by Maurice Seymour.

Festival Ballet entitled *Vilia* in 1952, and the music was not well arranged for a ballet. Markova is not the kind of dancer who comes out on the stage and stuns the audience with brilliant fireworks. She is delicate and fragile looking (but with a body made of steel; she even knocked my big husband off his feet when he said something she did not like), and despite her ethereal quality she has a sense of tongue-in-cheek comedy. This was our cue for the interpretation of her *Widow*. In her first entrance she wore a brilliant red costume all covered with diamonds, red feathers in her hair. This might have looked vulgar on anyone else, but not with Markova. She was the last word in Parisian chic, and had at the same time a tiny touch of Fanny Brice. The combination was delicious.

For her second entrance in the Garden Scene, Rolf Gerard (our designer) dressed her in a knee-length Marsovian style ballet dress with a cute small hat. I choreographed for her a very fast, brilliant little pizzicato, in which her footwork looked miraculous. She came to visit me in St. Tropez to work on the Widow role, and it was in my studio there that I made this dance for her. Markova is very lazy (at least she was in St. Tropez), and if she worked an hour she felt that was enough. As she never danced full out in rehearsal, it was difficult for me to tell how the dance would turn out. We used to go to the beach right after rehearsal. Markova would always sit under a big umbrella, all wrapped up. She never went near the water and she always moved as little as possible. Her style was always understatement, and at this she was fantastically successful.

After Scene II, the Widow appears to Danilo in a dream (he lay on a couch in Maxims, having passed out after drinking too much champagne). She wore a little slip of a flowery costume, and she was about the most exquisite creature imaginable—like a will-o'-the-wisp and absolutely unforgettable—I can see her now.

In the finale Gerard gave Markova a white costume decorated with big pink roses and an enormous black hat, a combination of innocence and sophistication that was completely enchanting. As you can see, I couldn't have asked for anyone better in this role than Alicia. She is certainly not an easy person to deal with. When I sat with her and her smart sister on a business conversation with Carol Fox, I was glad that I was not Carol Fox! They are all three very shrewd. But after contracts were signed, Alicia's sister turned out to be extremely helpful. Alicia danced the *Widow* at Chicago Lyric Opera with the handsome Oleg Briansky, and they were certainly an exciting couple. We gave the *Widow* at the Broadway Theatre in New York for a week with the same cast, and it was at these performances that Columbia Artists saw my company and then arranged annual tours for us for the next fifteen years.

The same season Markova danced Leonore and Briansky Manrico in *Revenge*, my ballet version of *Il Trovatore*, with scenery and costumes by Antoni Clavé. This ballet created such a scandal with the Italian element of the Chicago Lyric Opera that, in spite of the fact that *Revenge* was a smash hit in Paris with the Ballet des Champs-Elysées and later in New York with my own company, we still could never perform it again in Chicago. Oh, Chicago!

Father Mitchell [1972]

Arthur Mitchell is both intelligent and charming, and he knows it. Arthur has a cause, and his cause is going to work. Most people thought blacks could never become ballet dancers, but Mitchell and his associate artistic director, Karel Shook, are proving that they can. Blacks have always been great performers, but they never had ballet training at the proper age, and even if they had, there would have been practically no companies in which they could get jobs.

As Lincoln Kirstein's protégé, Arthur was an exception, and for a long time he danced the ballets of George Balanchine and was an outstanding principal dancer with the New York City Ballet. So of course he is Balanchine-oriented. Katherine Dunham and Alvin Ailey have had black dance companies for years, based loosely on our native jazz, West Indian folklore, and modern dance, but Dance Theatre of Harlem is *real* ballet. Arthur has choreographed two ballets for that group in straight Balanchine style, *Fête Noire* (music by Shostakovitch) and *Holberg Suite* (music by Grieg), but he has also proved that he is a choreographer in his own right with *Rhythmetron* and *Biosfera* by Marlos Nobre, *Tones* by Tania Leon, and *Ode* by Coleridge Taylor Perkins. I hope he will not be so busy managing his company that he will no longer find time to choreograph more and to dance himself.

Arthur is a real father to his dancers. It is touching to see how carefully and thoughtfully he looks after them, and they are in turn devoted to him. They have no contracts and no union, and I hope they never will. They are going fine, and I enjoyed every minute of my work with them.

I went to Spoleto, Italy, where they were performing for three weeks in June and July (1972) for the Festival dei due Mondi. I hoped to get my ballet for them (*Carmen*) at least half finished, but I had so little time that I became frustrated and

Arthur Mitchell in rehearsal with two Dance Theatre of Harlem dancers. Photo by Marbeth.

extremely unhappy. However, I did enjoy getting acquainted with the company. They are very individual with all kinds of backgrounds—Aruba, Puerto Rico, Cuba, Harlem, California, and so on. Such sympathetic, lovable people, one could write a book about each of them. I was happy working with them and talking to them. I only wish I could have had more rehearsal time. After their successful opening night— even though the Italians are a difficult ballet audience—they decided to put *Agon* on their second program, and this is a difficult ballet for *any* company. I couldn't rehearse until it was finished, and this took most of their time. Arthur even had to fly with his assistant to Berlin to learn some of the corps steps from Patricia Neary. But what Arthur wants, Arthur gets, and *Agon* came off very well indeed in spite of a much less than perfect orchestra.

Arthur Mitchell is a person with no vices. He doesn't smoke or drink, and he eats lots of ice cream. He works very hard and is truly a splendid example for his young dancers. He is really a sort of Sir Galahad; "His strength is as the strength of ten because his heart is pure." The atmosphere is healthy and exceptional in every way. Mrs. Gimbel has just given the company a new building in Harlem with *three* studios. This will be a big help, as they have been rehearsing in an uncomfortable church. But these people do not need much help—it is a do-it-yourself group that will go far. Arthur, Karel, *all* of them are irresistible.

Rudi Is Always Tops [1971]

No one will ever have to take care of Rudolf Nureyev. He knows how to get along anyplace. It is extraordinary how quickly he was able to adjust to the free world. Of course the dance world is a place apart, and a dancer is always a dancer, no matter what country he happens to be in. There is a kind of universal club, with no headquarters and no dues, where all of us seem welcome and understanding of each other.

I met Nureyev with Margot Fonteyn in Nervi, Italy, not long after he defected. I often wonder what would have happened to Rudi if Margot had not befriended him and had not made of their partnership such a dazzling union. His other great friend, Erik Bruhn, must have inspired him too. With these two superb artists to guide him, he could not go wrong. Erik is usually considered the top male dancer of Europe, but not long after Rudi had danced in only a few places, the two of them came to St. Tropez to see me. They were riding in a small open car and the Tropezians of the port recognized Rudi right away, shouting his name and following the car, and no one even noticed the equally great but less sensational Danish star. My studio in St. Tropez had been inundated by the sea and we sat in the middle of it in a rowboat; there were even a few mushrooms growing in the floor. We were all laughing at our plight. Rudi wanted to practice (he is a hard worker), but with his first leaps, the floor caved in and he finally had to give up. We had to make a whole new floor.

In Russia, I suppose, Rudi was just one of many fine dancers, but here his technique plus his sheer animal magnetism swept us all off our feet. We had not seen a star like this for a long time—maybe never. His first appearance in the United States was with my Chicago Opera Ballet at the Brooklyn Academy of Music in 1962, and I

Rudolf Nureyev with Tom Fisher in Nervi, 1962. Photo by Lido.

(Above): Rudolf Nureyev and Sonia Arova in a performance of *Merry Widow,* 1962. *(Below):* Curtain calls for *Merry Widow* with Sonia Arova, Neal Kayan, Ruth Page and Nureyev, 1962. *(Right):* Sonia Arova and Rudolf Nureyev with members of the Chicago Opera Ballet and Ruth Page in rehearsal, 1962. Photos by Nancy Sorensen.

199

remember he was paid $500 for that performance! He and Sonia Arova, a member of my company, danced the old chestnut from *Don Quixote*, but they did it so brilliantly that one forgave him for his choice of pas de deux.

That was a strange night. My spotlight man was ill, so I had to spend the entire evening at the top of the balcony directing a new operator. One of my star dancers was ill and couldn't dance and there had to be a couple of changes for the corps. But it couldn't have mattered less, as everyone came only to see Rudi. Arova danced just as brilliantly as he did, but one hardly knew she was there. Certainly the best trained dancers in the world are the Russians, and Pushkin, Rudi's teacher, was the renowned professor of the male dancers in Leningrad.

Rudi is not particularly prepossessing as far as looks are concerned. His legs are short (I will never understand how he was able to partner tall girls so skillfully), and he is not good looking in the conventional sense. When Igor Youskevitch just stood still he was so arresting that *every* eye was riveted on him, but Rudi has to be in motion. When he takes to the air, he is of course breathtaking. His domain will always be the air, and he needs lots of space to show himself to best advantage.

Nureyev's second appearance in the United States was with the Chicago Lyric Opera in an all-ballet evening. He danced Prince Danilo in my *Merry Widow* with Sonia Arova. This is not a ballet to show a dancer's virtuosity, but his smooth, aristocratic dancing and acting made *him* the star of this ballet rather than the Widow. Even though he has a Russian peasant background, he was every inch a spoiled prince.

He also danced the Danish *Flower Festival Pas de Deux* on the same program, and his youthful ballon was captivating. He didn't like the costume that I had inherited from Flemming Flindt (who had danced the same pas de deux the year before), and he started to throw it out the window into the river. I grabbed it just in time, and while I saw to it that he got a costume that pleased him, I certainly didn't see any point in throwing Flemming Flindt's excellent costume into the river. The only time I ever saw a costume being treated so rudely was when I was with the Ballets des Champs-Elysées in Paris and Violette Verdy's mother tore up a costume so that her daughter would not have to wear it. I often wonder what would happen to a dancer in Russia if he started destroying a costume, and some of *their* costumes really *should* be destroyed! One of my favorite dancers tore up one of my costumes at the end of our last tour, and I have not spoken to her since.

That same season, the Chicago Lyric Opera produced *Prince Igor* with Boris Christoff heading a magnificent cast and with our own great chorus singing in Russian. Alexandre Benois designed the appropriate scenery and costumes, and Rudi danced the chief warrior with Sonia Arova as the Polovetsian girl and Dolores Lipinski as the wild Polovetsian boy. I wanted the ballet to be as close to Fokine's original choreography as possible, as this ballet is one of his masterpieces. Rudy had his costume cut so that his middle was bare, and he used more spectacular, athletic steps than Fokine had used. His animal quality as usual reached across the footlights, as he jumped higher and higher. My only criticism was that he stopped in between his great leaps to get his breath, and I don't think Fokine would have approved of that. Anyway, it was a thrilling performance.

Rudi stayed with me while he was rehearsing and dancing in Chicago. He is one of the easiest house guests I ever had. As long as he got a steak, plenty of tea, a little whiskey, a massage, a game of chess (which he played with my husband), and a telephone call to Erik in Australia, he was very undemanding. His telephone bill was over $1,000, which he paid immediately!

Rudi is a truly great artist. He is hard on his partners (as he is on himself), and he insists always on perfection. He has at his command all the old Russian repertoire, and what a splendid background that is! He seems to have a fabulous memory, and what he doesn't remember I suppose (like Balanchine) he makes up.

Like most Russians, Rudi is a warm, sympathetic person. Women and men both love him—you can't help loving him. His hair is so soft and thick and such a lovely honey color.

Rudi has become a sort of social lion. He likes to drink and carouse around after his performances at night, but I don't think he will ever let anything or anybody seriously interfere with his art. What an inspiration he has been to all of us. He must have lots of love affairs and I'm sure he's always tops!

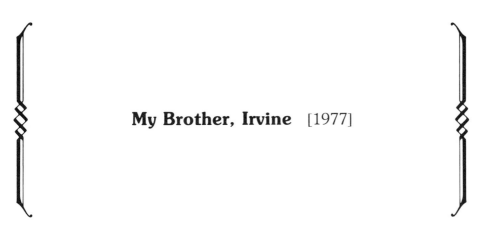

My Brother, Irvine [1977]

What is the extraordinary relationship of brother and sister usually like? As a young girl, I admired my older brother Lafayette, because he was good-looking, pugnacious, and he took me to proms at Princeton (where he was a very bad student and drank a lot). He introduced me to all of his most attractive friends and then left me alone to have a good time with anyone I chose.

My older brother, Irvine, was entirely different. While Lafayette was out of town always getting himself into trouble, Irvine stayed home with his microscopes, looking at God knows what, and his room was so filled with bottles, that I was afraid to go in there for fear everything would blow up. Also he didn't like to be disturbed! Irvine had beautiful auburn hair and pensive dark eyes. Virginia Keep was doing a portrait of him, and mother and I were in the room trying hard to entertain him with all kinds of silly ideas when finally he said, "Oh mother, let's just sit here and fink (think)."

We went every summer to our cottage in Hyannisport. We children watched so many beautiful boats on the horizon and in the harbor that we decided we *must* have a yacht. So, every day we went to the woods and picked blueberries and blackberries to sell, so that we could have money to buy a yacht. Our favorite "yacht" was an old yawl which anchored at the pier. Captain Slokum had been all around the world *alone,* except for a cat, in this small boat and he had made a glorious collection of seashells, sea fans, and all the strange exotica from the sea. Maybe this is what set off Irvine to start a collection of seaweeds, while his friend Shields Warren specialized in seashells. The collection grew and grew and finally the two little boys got quite a reputation, and were asked to show their work to a Dr. Collins, a famous expert on the subject, at a meeting of algologists in Chatham. Dr. Collins and his laboratory expected to see two grown men, and when the two little boys showed up, everyone was flabbergasted.

After we grew up, I didn't see much of Irvine. He was completely engrossed in the world of science and medicine. He was twice president of the American Heart Association, director of research at the Cleveland Clinic and director of the chemical division of The Kaiser Wilhelm Institute in Munich, Germany. He took all the awards you ever heard of. I was going to list them but his secretary just sent me three pages of listings plus all ten books he has written, so I gave up. No wonder he had no time for me. And my world was a complete contrast—the mad insane world of ballet. But when I see him now I am impressed with his humanity, his candor and his honesty. I always read his essays (he was editor of *Modern Medicine* for sixteen years and is now editor emeritus) consisting of two pages chuck-full of ideas on every subject. He always seems to hit the nail on the head!

The philosophy and psychology of the child mind is usually hard to fathom. My older brother Lafayette accepted the world as he saw it and I did somewhat the same. Not so Irvine. One day at Hyannisport our father said that if the weather was good he would take us sailing. Lafayette scanned the skies and said the weather was going to be fine. I agreed but Irvine remarked very philosophically "Well you never can tell what God is going to do." I must confess the management up there in its control of the weather hasn't changed much.

HEART DISEASE
What the Doctors Say

TIME

THE WEEKLY NEWSMAGAZINE

DR. IRVINE PAGE,
HEART SPECIALIST

William Vandivert

Dr. Irvine Page. Photo by William Vandivert.

Always a realist, Irvine bought an all-day sucker and was furious when it only sucked till eleven o'clock. Consumer protection at that time was unborn.

But isn't it great that we are all so different! On that most people would agree, and that God in some insensible way has made a great success of it, and all without government subsidy or an academic degree.

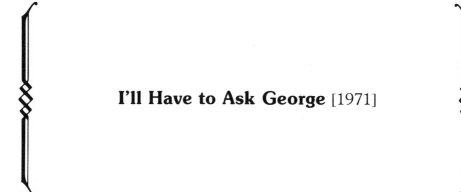

I'll Have to Ask George [1971]

Marjorie Tallchief is a quiet person. If you ask her something, no matter what, she always says, "Well, I'll have to ask George" (her husband, George Skibine). She never says a word at rehearsals, and she does whatever you tell her without any questions, and does it quickly, easily and beautifully. I never quite understood what Maria Tallchief meant when she once said to me, "Poor Marjorie, she has no technique." Perhaps she does not have the crisp, hard, exact attack of a Balanchine dancer, but she has strength, a fluid line, high extensions, and a poetic quality all her own that I find enchantingly irresistible. She can also do all kinds of stunts if required.

Marjorie Tallchief is distinguished looking but not a pretty girl off stage, but on stage she is radiantly beautiful. I do not think she has had the big success she deserves. She and her attractive husband went on several tours with my Chicago Opera Ballet, and they danced and acted sympathetically and brilliantly in my *Merry Widow, Revenge,* and *Camille.*

We gave a performance of *Camille* in Fairfax, Oklahoma, the Tallchiefs' home town, and Marjorie's father saw her dance for the first time. I thought she gave an especially heartwarming performance as Camille. I went up to her father (a big, impressive-looking Indian), all enthusiasm, and said to him, "Wasn't Marjorie great? Wasn't she enchanting? What did you think of your daughter?" All he answered was, "Ugh." Very Indian, I suppose.

George Skibine and Marjorie Tallchief in *Camille.*

Dearest Van [1972]

My letters to Isaac Van Grove always begin the same way, "Dearest Van," and I can't begin to count the times I have written to him. We have collaborated on about a dozen ballets, and we did them almost entirely by correspondence. The one or two times that we have been together I hardly knew how to talk to him or he to me. All the other artists I have worked with will say, "I'll work with you if we can meet and talk, but I can't do anything by correspondence."

I would of course prefer to be with any artist with whom I collaborate, but writing out all your ideas and thoughts has many advantages. Everything is clarified and there is no chance of being sloppy and vague. Once you have worked with Van Grove, it is difficult to change to anyone else. I notice Paul Green always uses him to arrange and compose the music for his pageants, which always seem so successful. Van Grove has composed several operas for his students and has a reputation as a great operatic coach. He always has the music you want ready on time (which believe me is rare), even though he is a busy person. Here is a quote from his last letter to me, dated August 12, 1972:

The Inspiration season (The Fine Arts Colony at Inspiration Point, Eureka Springs, Arkansas) was successful in terms of accomplishments by some 70 singers, and a dozen or so of them quite unusual. We did *Rigoletto* (4 of them with 4 Gildas); *Don Giovanni*, with a tremendously talented bass baritone, Paul Geiger from the Chicago area, who needs but a push by an "affluent" sponsor to go to Germany and become a "somebody" in opera; 4 *Don Giovanni* shows with 4 Zerlinas, 2 Donna Annas, 3 Donna Elviras (you can imagine the effort to train these young folk). We did *Down in the Valley* (Weill), 4 of them with 4 different casts, Joan [Van Grove]'s headache, though she is marvelous in staging these tyros, and my new opus, *The Miracles of Our Lady*, which seemed to have made quite an impression on cast, shows and public. I plan to extend it by 4 intermediate scenes which explains dramatically and *visually* the decadence of the nun during the 20 years she lived in the world.

So *Alice* is out for next spring, leaving a gap in your plans, which I suspect from experience that you will fill with alternatives. Yes, Chicago is an uncertain city, never having recovered

Isaac Van Grove.

from the most lethal blow dealt by the depression . . . Still it is a wonderful city, but without pride in its own. What you have done for the town should be appreciated and encouraged. Can we hope the time will come for a change for the better? Maybe another depression? And an equivalent of a WPA? (The last one gave us the only local performing companies, you remember.)

My first collaboration with Van Grove was *Revenge*, the fifty-minute ballet based on Verdi's *Il Trovatore*. Dearest Van knows all the operas inside out, as he was with the Chicago Opera during the great days of Mary Garden. His fund of stories about this period could fill a book. But, unlike most opera people, his mind is not closed to liberal use of operatic music. Obviously neither the libretto nor the music of an opera can be used exactly as written, so one has to cut and rearrange and decide what music is suitable for dancing. Strangely enough, most operatic music is appropriate for ballet, and the dancing body easily takes the place of the singing voice. You just can't make dances quite as long as songs. Verdi's opera music is great for dancing, but the music he wrote for ballet is uninspiring, almost insipid.

Revenge was an immediate hit at its premiere in Paris, but when we gave it the following fall with Chicago Lyric Opera, it was such a scandal! Dear, marvelous, old conductor Serafin nearly died of shock, but the intelligentsia found the idea of Callas singing Leonora in the opera, and Markova dancing Leonora in the ballet, very intriguing. Anyway, *Revenge* was the beginning of a series of operas made into ballets, and they were really all successful.

I wanted to get away from the short divertissement style of ballet programs and have only two ballets for the entire evening. My husband suggested the *Merry Widow*. I frankly didn't like the idea much, but I did think it would go well on the same program with *Revenge*. My first version, *Vilia*, for the London Festival Ballet, had a musical arrangement by Van Grove, but it was not ideal as a production because at that time you could not make changes of scenery at the Festival Hall, and we had to leave out the whole Marsovian scene, so there was too much waltzing.

We had a difficult time getting the rights to use the *Merry Widow* music and libretto. Finally, I took a chance and we opened in Manchester, England, on Franz Lehár's birthday. His heirs came to Manchester to see the performance, and we all heaved a sigh of relief when they were so enthusiastic they said, "This ballet version should make a whole new life for the *Widow*." At this time Hassard Short came into the picture, and he suggested Hans May (a real Viennese of the Lehár school) to rework the music. We spent all summer in Europe working on the new score as well as on new costumes and scenery. Georges Wakhevitch had designed the London version, but we got Rolf Gerard for the American version (with both New York Karinska and Paris Karinska working on the execution of the costumes).

Even after all this work, the music was not quite what we wanted. So Van Grove worked on our third orchestral version, and finally we were ready to go. We performed it for a week in New York in the Broadway Theatre with Alicia Markova and Oleg Briansky, at the Chicago Lyric Opera with the same cast, and later at the Chicago Lyric Opera with Rudolf Nureyev and Sonia Arova. And from then on we toured with it for years.

Following the *Widow*, I did *Salome* with Van Grove. Again we had difficulties with the musical rights. Fortunately Van Grove had a letter from Richard Strauss congratulating him on his splendid performance as conductor for Mary Garden's *Salome*, so we somehow managed to get permission. However, I never really performed this ballet because we couldn't afford a large enough orchestra and the subject matter was not appropriate for touring. It was one of my favorite ballets and I liked the scenery and costumes that Nicholas Remisoff designed (completely unoperatic). After *Salome* we collaborated on *Susanna and the Barber* of Rossini with enchanting sets and costumes by Antoni Clavé, also unoperatic, but this ballet had a great deal of dialogue in it and so was not practical for touring.

Our next ballet together was *Carmen*, of which I have now done four versions, the first one with John Pratt and Clive Rickabaugh, one with Nicholas Remisoff, one with Bernard Daydé, and the fourth with André Delfau (1972), and this is my last.

Our most successful opera-into-ballet was *Camille* (based on Verdi's *La Traviata*). This story is of course a natural for ballet, and Van Grove's arrangement of the music is perfect.

Van Grove had a brilliant idea for a ballet I wanted to choreograph on the subject of Mephistopheles. Our libretto was loosely based on Heinrich Heine's fascinating *Dr. Faustus, a dance poem*. This story had to be greatly simplified, as our United States tours just can't accommodate big, elaborate productions. But Van Grove's idea was to take three romantic composers who had written opera about the devil and use one composer for each scene: Gounod, Boito, and Berlioz. The idea worked like a dream, although some music critics complained. But I used this ballet for only one tour as I couldn't use all the stage tricks that I needed for this idea. I am dying to do it again. Delfau's scenery and costumes are superb, and they should not be packed away in a storeroom.

Van Grove and I did only one nonoperatic ballet, called *Combinations*. Van Grove composed the music on one theme with lots of clever variations and ideas. I particularly liked the dance of the telephones. We did a short version of *Pygmalion*, and we are still discussing other ideas.

I really can't think of anything wrong with "Dearest Van." He even has a perfectly lovely wife whom I adore and who is a talented director. They are both self-effacing and never push, so they are relatively unknown. Anyway, they are loved and appreciated by *me*.

Gripes [1972]

My dancers never stop complaining. Floors are always too slippery and too hard (and on this point they have my complete sympathy), theatres are always too cold (I usually suffocate), they hate to meet people and sign autographs and go to parties (I find most parties interesting for all kinds of reasons, mainly, perhaps, for insights into human nature). Dancers just like to sit down after performances and eat (admittedly the most comfortable thing to do). They hate all company managers except Jeannot Cerrone and Philippe de Conville, and they hate Columbia Artists because it books tours with trips too long between cities. (Do they know that the United States is a *very large* country?) They hate the bus and they hate even worse a big limousine seating eight people which we took for our lecture tour in 1971. I called it the Black Dragon because it really swallowed us up.

They complained for fifteen years at the opera because there never was enough space to dance full out, and they never had enough to do (I certainly understood this). Practically no dancer in the whole world likes to dance in opera—although I enjoyed it in my dancing days because I always managed to choreograph good parts for myself *and* I was interested in the challenge that choreographing for opera poses.

My dancers moan and groan before they dance and during class, and every night we have a battle over the rosin. The ballerinas want *every* inch of the stage completely covered, and the male dancers don't want any at all. Toe shoes being a slippery, dangerous invention, I think I side with the girls on this point. When there were no footlights they wanted them, and when there *were* footlights they couldn't see. When we gave five performances a week they were bored on the two free days; if we gave six a week they were exhausted. To tell the truth, dancers are not happy *unless* they are complaining. Yet curiously, they seem to have fun and a sense of humor. I really think they hate to dance, yet they are superb dancers, and when they come out on stage you would never know they had been through such torture. And so their lives pass waiting for—what? Those perfect conditions which so rarely if ever happen?

Patricia Klekovic and Charles Schick in *Carmina Burana*.

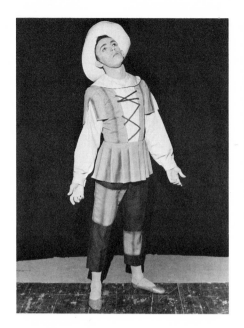

(Above): Larry Long and Dolores Lipinski in the Lyric Opera production of *Carmina Burana,* choreography by Ruth Page, 1965. *(Below):* Orrin Kayan and Patricia Klekovic in Ruth Page's *Carmen,* costumes by Daydé.

Kenneth Johnson and Patricia Klekovic in Ruth Page's *Catulli Carmina,* costumes by Delfau.

Kenneth Johnson was an exception and always seemed to enjoy dancing both at rehearsals and in class. He started a little too late to have a brilliant classical technique, but he had a great natural talent and was always as smooth as silk. His renversé turns and backward arabesque pirouettes were better than anyone else's. He became a fine dancing actor and a great partner. I used to love to work on lifts with him. To be a good partner you have to like being a cavalier. So many male dancers hate to lift. But a good part of their job, especially in classic ballets, is to make a ballerina look light and airy and beautiful, and this requires a lot of strength and know-how.

Kenneth could partner almost anyone. The only one I ever heard him complain about was Melissa Hayden, and it seems that all the boys have difficulty with her, as she seems to like to lead her partner rather than allow the partner to lead her. Melissa usually had her way, but she always ended up looking great. She and Kenneth were truly exciting as the tragic lovers in my ballet *Camille.* I enjoyed working with Ken more than any other of my dancers, because his attitude was always cooperative and sympathetic.

213

Patricia Klekovic is one of the most poetic, exquisite dancers I've ever seen—stubborn as a mule, unbending in her morals, matter of fact in life, unimaginative, but a dreamy dancer. She is slow to tackle a new role, but when she finally takes over, every detail is thoroughly worked out and her interpretations are profound and moving. She hates to move fast and small, always balking at any kind of allegro work. Dancing was always difficult for her, but through the help of her teacher, Edna McRae, she surmounted almost all difficulties.

Her background was limited, and I thought that a trip to Europe might enlarge her horizons. But I was wrong; it didn't help at all. André Delfau, who is an inspired guide, introduced her to the wonders of Paris, but she didn't seem to see. What really impressed her was St. Peter's in Rome. Patricia is a truly religious girl, and big tears flowed from her eyes when St. Peter's was revealed to her. She was extremely disappointed that the catacombs were closed due to strikes and none of the museums in Florence were open either. However, she seemed to enjoy Italy, especially the parties that Arthur Cummings and Dan Arensky had for us in their lovely villa.

She had several suitors, but she always remained chaste. I took her to St. Tropez with me, but she doesn't like the sea or swimming or the sun, so she was not very happy there.

I often think that when her stage career is over she will become a good, conscientious, careful teacher of ballet, but I doubt if she will ever "live" except in dance. Anyway, I was completely satisfied with her in all my ballets—I think she loved most of the roles I gave her. Our collaboration was always successful. What she needs now is a passionate lover who will make her flower into the beauty she should be.*

Dancing was difficult for *Dolores Lipinski* too, for, like Patricia Klekovic, she was a big girl. But she learned to dance magnificently (her teachers were Stone-Camryn) and developed into a splendid artist. She hated touring and suffered unsilently. I think she would like to dance mostly straight classical roles. She likes being home in the Middle West, and she doesn't like Europe because "it isn't America." She likes domestic comforts and stylish clothes. From the look of her picture collection, Dolores's ideal American male is Paul Newman, but you couldn't find a more devoted wife. I adore her not only because she dances so well, but because she doesn't try to be anything she isn't. As a character she is unique, entertaining, and unpretentious. She looks voluptuous and tempting, but at heart she seems puritanical. She married Larry Long while they were both on tour in my company.

* Patricia Klekovic is now happily married to Rodney Irwin and they are both teaching brilliantly at the Ruth Page Foundation School.

Larry Long says I took him into my company because he could do "butterflies." He started in my corps de ballet, then became a soloist and choreographer, and finally successfully filled the most difficult of all jobs, ballet master. Now he is Director of the Ruth Page Foundation school. I have complete confidence in his talent and abilities and hope that our association will be long and fruitful. I wish he were my son!

Neal and Orrin Kayan were born with perfect dancing bodies. Neal was my long-time musical collaborator, starting as pianist and ending up as conductor, orchestrator, and sometimes composer. How I wish I could have afforded the orchestra he deserved! He was so sensitive to dance that we never had any tempi or musical trouble with him of any kind until he and Kenneth Johnson split up their friendship. Then rehearsals became nightmares. But usually we kept personal problems to ourselves.

Edna McRae gave Orrin Kayan a correct technique. Edna was a teacher who *made* her pupils work, or they had to get out. Oh, how hard she worked. I never thought Chicago really appreciated what a great teacher she was. I received an inadequate training at the beginning of my career, but *fortunately* I went to Edna when I came to Chicago, and she straightened me out on many problems. Orrin is naturally lazy physically, and he needed the push that Edna gave him. He is a born dance comedian but does not like to do comic roles. Like Klekovic and Lipinski he is a rather conventional person, and it is sometimes difficult for me to open up new horizons for them. They knew all the rules and did not like to break them.

Orrin above all liked to eat, drink, and make love, and I felt that sometimes he liked to "live" too much for the good of his dancing. He liked to overdo the drinking and the loving, but I never thought he overdid enough on his dancing. One class a day was enough for him. He was conscientious in rehearsals, but never wanted to branch out into roles that he imagined he could never do. He admired and adored Henning Kronstam (so did I), and Henning strengthened Orrin's technique and gave him good artistic advice.

Charles Schick was important to me as a dancer. He understood my style so intuitively and he was exactly what I wanted for the leading role in my ballet *Carmina Burana*. He was forceful, strong, and uninhibited, and I worked out many pas de deux with him. *I* liked him as a partner, but my ballerinas found him rough, not smooth and attentive like Kenneth. He was never a straight classical dancer and although I worked out my pas de deux for the Snow Scene in *Nutcracker* on him, he could never do the solo stunts well enough.

He was a delicious comedian, but like so many artists who have talent along a certain line, he wanted to do something else. In his heart I think he would have liked to be a classical dancer, but his feet were not right and he was inclined to be heavy. Yet he never really wanted to do the parts in which he was so great. I will never forget him as Dr. Falke in *Die Fledermaus*. He was an ideal master of ceremonies and his sense of comedy and timing held the whole ballet together.

Most of these dancers were with me a long time (fifteen years) and I loved them and was interested in all their problems. They developed into real artists, and when we had to disband the company it was a real tragedy for us. How I wish I could have given them a weekly salary all the year round, a good floor to dance on, a large orchestra, and so on. I *did* give them first-class productions and saw to it that they always were costumed to perfection. If we only had in Chicago half of what the European companies have, we would have been able to have continuous ballet performances in Chicago and I never would have to lose them.

Index

Index